solstice
TO solstice
TO solstice

solstice TO solstice TO solstice

A Year of *sunrises* in Poetry

ALLISON BOYD JUSTUS

Alternating Current
Boulder, Colorado

Solstice to Solstice to Solstice
Allison Boyd Justus
©2017 Alternating Current Press

All material in *Solstice to Solstice to Solstice* is the property of its respective creator and may not be used or reprinted in any manner without express permission from the author or publisher, except for the quotation of short passages used inside of an article, criticism, or review. Printed in the United States of America. All rights reserved. All material in *Solstice to Solstice to Solstice* is printed with permission.

Alternating Current
Boulder, Colorado
alternatingcurrentarts.com

ISBN-10: 1-946580-01-5
ISBN-13: 978-1-946580-01-6
First Edition: March 2017

TO STEVE AND CAROL BOYD—

Thank you for letting me grow up
with real trees and a view of the mountain
and for your unending love.

AND TO DANA—

Thank you for understanding music and asymptotes,
and for pointing me to Midtown.

advance praise

"Justus gives us 366 mornings of sunrises during a single solar year, 366 blank slates, 366 chances to perceive and create something new. These eye-opening poems are like mornings themselves, full of startling pleasures: 'light brilliant as fact,' 'the mountain a shudder,' 'a murmuration of starlings rattl[ing] like a tambourine.' Justus shows us that each day is a page where anything might be written."
—Maggie Smith, author of *The Well Speaks of Its Own Poison*

"Justus reminds us that observation is one of the most important parts of being alive: just noting change and presence. She forces attention to the small things, and even though the sky is the star, the speaker takes on a supporting role. By the end, it seems that both the sun and the speaker have learned something in their year: they're back where they started, but also further along. There's something about witnessing dawn, each day—knowing, this is new, and untouched."
—Micah Ling, author of *Sweetgrass*, *Settlement*, and *Flashes of Life*

"Justus chronicles one year's worth of sunrises, from one December 21st to the next, a document that is as much prayerlike supplication as it is physical phenomenon. Each morning takes shape, almost insecure about its inevitable happening: our counter-course reading from left to right orients us as Justus' writing dispels the dark."
—Anthony Michael Morena, author of *The Voyager Record*

"When I was younger, I imagined I would be a quirky nature writer who juxtaposed philosophical questions with whatever oddities I found in the creek. At some point, I turned into a person who wakes up at night worrying about course substitution forms. So it goes. Justus took the right path. Who wakes up every day and watches the sunrise? The person I'd like to be. So I got up twice and watched the sunrise. Twice in a row. Many books have changed the way I think, but none have inspired me to get up before 6 a.m., until this one. What Justus finds in sunrises is a conversation between those soft-spoken lights and her own sense of wonder. The pleasure of this book is stumbling into that conversation, and listening as if you shouldn't. It is the same thrill of overhearing people at another table speak about how they should try again, how there is still a chance, how the sun will rise again the next day and offer something unexpected."
—Gregory Robinson, author of *All Movies Love the Moon*

"Justus squeezes a lot of light out of each dawn."
—Charles P. Ries, author of *Girl Friend & Other Mysteries of Love*

"Justus performs magic through visceral imagery in her mesmerizing collection. She sets her sights inside and outside each morning where the brilliance resides."

—Meg Tuite, author of *Bound by Blue*

"What a daunting achievement for Justus—a full year of waking mornings to shape poetic reactions for our dawning planet. The tension between what her eyes and senses make of dawn and her knowledge that earth is spinning 18.5 miles a second around a star is central to this book. Justus also knows that, at the same time, the red fringe at the edge of the universe is rushing toward *somethingness*, and that we are in the presence of a cosmic force beyond human comprehension. Yet she maintains a transcendental trust in the human imagination and her personal intuitive vision that grows from a deep sense of wonder. Her responses range from dawn snatches, to yawning wakefulness, to complete poems and inventive personal commentary: from rushed city mornings loud with traffic and train whistles, to the sun, a rose, rising above mountains and rivers. What every entry has in common is the gift of language—witty, sensory rich, poetic, and often prayerful. For Justus each dawn brings new birth into this life, this gift."

—Bill Brown, author of *Elemental* and *Morning Window*

"Gorgeous lyrical prosody and wonderful concept."

—Tiana Clark, author of *Equilibrium*

"There may only be two solstices a year, but Justus reminds us that every day gives birth to poetry. These pieces are full of vivid imagery and keen observations that prove that regardless of the sun's position in the sky, you can always be illuminated. A perfect collection to leave at your bedside and read each morning before heading into your day."

—Rebecca Schumejda, author of *Waiting at the Dead End Diner*

"'The days aren't endless and you've got to build them into something,' Justus reminds us. She does just that, transforming one year into a catalog of sunrises, a directory of documented dawns. Probing and relentlessly inquisitive, her fragmented vignettes peer through the window of the ordinary, squinting into the light. These poems are miniature yet muscular meditations on darkness, change, safety, stillness, and time."

—Hannah Stephenson, author of *In the Kettle, the Shriek*

"The task of the poet is to be a watcher of the world, and Justus takes to the task with precision and joy. Like the sunrise itself, these poems are deceptive in their simplicity, both stilling and stirring in their music, and wondrous in their ability to take our breath away."

—Marc Beaudin, author of *Vagabond Song*

"'Solipsism won't do,' writes Justus, as she turns toward a consciousness that is beyond our individual experience. Just as the title's astronomical event connects itself to the equinoxes and the seasons of the year, Justus' poetry connects us through a shared history by observing with careful patience the passing of time and its eternal resonance. Addressing Thoreau and Dickinson, Picasso and Escher, Justus creates a world filled with moments of humor as well as artistic and philosophical inquiry into what it means to be acutely aware of our own mortality—spinning toward our own death and an unnamable power beyond ourselves. The speaker is always holding onto something—the light, the water, the air—and it all rises into song, one that holds us—and reminds us—that it is nice to 'like to sit with possibilities,' acknowledging all the beauty of where we are, as well as appreciating the unknown to where we are headed."

—John McCarthy, author of *Ghost County*

"'The clock's struck winter, and the marble's at the bottom of the bowl.' So begins Justus' journey of sunrises and salutations, simplicities and complexities, observations and meditations. If 'Winter begins small [...] kept in a tight fist,' this collection does anything but, layering concrete, vital images between personal insights. Justus isn't satisfied with simply documenting a year of sunrises; she's willing to be taught, to see within and beyond the morning into herself, her world, and its mysteries. As the year turns day by sunlit day, Justus pulls the essential from the darkness with a measured hand, a hand that will not give 'what you do not actually need.' In the end, this poet proclaims what is necessary, what is needed, with a voice bright as a new morning—'And what do I need? To be shot through: to be shot through with light.' Yes. Exactly. It's what we all need. And it's what we find in this luminous collection."

—Sandy Coomer, author of *The Presence of Absence*

"'Rise to remember what could be forgotten, and water it,' writes Justus, and that's exactly what she's done for a year and a day. In these pages 'the sun's around here somewhere' with the visual glory you'd expect—tangerines, sherbets, lavenders—but these poems are also a place where the 'groggy body' is invited to listen: to silence and stillness, to clouds and questions, to math and science, to lyric whimsy punctuated with straightforward confessions of shortcomings and pain. This poet's world is one where the grass grows, onions first; where atoms are tiny pearls; where a heating-and-air unit hums with stories; where sunlight can be ornery; and where what's most wanted is 'grounds for wild hope.' Whether you read these daily missives as poems, devotions, or instructions for paying better attention, you're sure to find that 'joy will come around.'"

—Kory Wells, author of *Heaven Was the Moon*

"Justus measures each day's dawning with the precision of a watch-maker. In an age when data geeks are the lords of everything, Justus' plums of truth deliver: 'Live in a light house, and frugally,' and 'Must I force everything open?' Begun on a Winter Solstice, the collection seems to spring out of an urge to mark the bare-bones December mornings, but the revelations come in a year of sunrises. Her talent lies in conjuring the cache of life in 366 altogether different overtures, find-ing divine purpose in nature alongside the ordinary. Like Whitman before her, Justus brings a way of seeing connection between self and nature, but like William Carlos Williams, all is viewed from her pri-vate vista: in her case, a window facing east."

—Andrea Mosier, author of *Fire Eater*

"Just as Maggie Nelson captivates with her book-length litany on love for a color in *Bluets*, Justus does the same with 366 sunrises. In descrip-tive passages the sunrise and dawn-seeker revolve, both in unison and in contradiction, like a long-term relationship struggling to find the original in the familiar. Here there 'are new beginnings, mercies / new-every-morning.' The dawn-seeker becomes intrinsically connected with the sky—in thirsty curiosity of the science '$y=mx+b$,' and by rejoicing 'o day, o dawning dance.' The craggy pear tree and various birdsongs remind that there is more than the sky, so much to see, and ample to remember within the meditative dialogues through the year: love, disappointment, joy, existentialism. Read it in total, or enjoy it in sections; Justus' passages will enchant."

—Catherine Moore, author of *Story* and *Wetlands*

"Justus explores a year's worth of sunrises in short, poetic vignettes that range from vibrant encapsulations of dawn to enigmatic fragments in which the reader encounters ghosts and hints of what lies beyond the edges of the work. The narrator greets each day from the kitchen, over cups of coffee, and it is against this quotidian backdrop that the reader sees dawn reinvented 366 times: through image, through physics, through memory, through aphorism. Justus writes, 'I like to sit with possibilities,' and this work invites the reader to do the same: to rise early and see where each moment will take her. The connection between the speaker and an elusive subject appears as do snippets of dream, the fleeting feeling of last night or years ago, appropriate for the stolen, in-between nature of crepuscular hours. Though seldom does the narrator invoke other people outright, there is a collective turn where she writes we, our, and it's impossible not to feel a part of each small, miraculous morning. Both contemplative and playful, *Solstice to Solstice to Solstice* keeps turning, and returning, to the light."

—Holly M. Wendt, American Antiquarian Society Award winner

The following collection documents the sunrises of one year, as observed by the poet, beginning with the 2009 winter solstice.

In June of 2010, the poet-observer relocates from Viola Road in McMinnville, Tennessee, to Upper Broadway in Nashville, with periodic visits to McMinnville and Manchester, Tennessee, during the transition and occasionally afterward.

Sunrise times noted throughout the collection are those computed by the U.S. Naval Observatory for McMinnville until June 3, and for Nashville thereafter. Daylight Saving Time begins March 14 and ends November 7.

If I say, "Surely the darkness shall cover me,
and the light about me be night,"
even the darkness is not dark to you;
the night is bright as the day,
for darkness is as light with you.

—PSALM 139:11-12

solstice
TO *solstice*
TO *solstice*

Not knowing when the Dawn will come,
I open every Door …

—EMILY DICKINSON

sunrise 1
6:49 A.M. DECEMBER 21

The clock's struck winter, and the marble's at the bottom of the bowl.

I rise while it is yet night.

Earth's ice-stark and bare and a thick secret blue, save for that fiery pink rim. If the horizon is a rim, half the planet's inverted, this hemisphere concave like a bowl. The other side is concave, too; its bowl is full of summer.

The first strong ray arrives (shoulders back, chin high) and pins itself onto the mountain.

sunrise 2
6:49 A.M. DECEMBER 22

The solstice falls at the end of the fall—rock bottom. Winter begins small, crushed, kept in a tight fist, and expands unto the equinox. This morning a purple cloud, low, horizontal, and rooflike, hovers just above the far trees.

I like to sit with possibilities. They gather 'round and gaze up at me, angel-eyed, expectant. I count the cups and saucers, and we all have tea.

sunrise 3
6:50 A.M. DECEMBER 23

Darling dawn a-dawning,
      dawn a-downing,
          down
    the coffee in the morning,
          morning meets the world a-spinning
        down
            toward the sun.

The sky stood dark and pre-dawnly. A light from inside the house shone out,   out onto a tree. The sun
hasn't yet risen; we're just shining our own poor light
out into it all. Shaky yellow manufactured meanings!
All the while the day dawns, strong and red.

sunrise 4
6:50 A.M. DECEMBER 24

The early morning thing is that the morning fire spread heralding.

The skin's awareness of gravity upon waking dredges
up with it nagging visions of another sky's reflection
     in an old lake. I walked alone
         to the lake to reclaim my access.
             Such vastness
               would not remain
                 beyond my reach.

The river, however, would not be reclaimed.
The soft stir of its waters on a still morning, perhaps; maybe
     the rush of its rapids; perhaps a short stretch of shore,
       for a time; maybe even
         the near-straight-shot path
           down to the wide bank
       —but the river I wanted has long since escaped.

sunrise 5
6:51 A.M. DECEMBER 25

I've come here to know, and I've come here to
fight the insistence that something essential is
missing (the absence that twists along inside the
sunrises and the hard questions and all the right
songs).

sunrise 6
6:51 A.M. DECEMBER 26

My powers of observation are, thus far, less than
acute. I'm blunted, but I get the job done: bare
trees' bare branches spread tangled and crazed,
black against butternut dawn.

sunrise 7
6:51 A.M. DECEMBER 27

involuntarily oriented:

this is the scene: We are facing the east.
Eastward we were driven from the garden,
and eastward we're rerouted every morning;
some large hand turns our tired faces that way,
         force-feeding us raw hope. So we are propelled east
with the current, with the earthspin, with the curse.

Spring's months away, yet
when it gets here, its young growth
will follow the arc of the sun all day, hungry—
and I, trained to hungrily synthesize light from some shining
false source, still stretch out and bend toward its arc,
which is no longer an arc,
but a snaking away
in the dark.

sunrise 8
6:52 A.M. DECEMBER 28

A backdrop:

The river wound away into the dark,
            and the darkness
      was holy and clear, celebrated with stars,
         streaked with Leonids.
       I stayed out the whole night,
   all talk and no fire,
    all yearning awe and
       expectation.

Past four we decided to wait for the sunrise,
      though we'd forgot
        which way was east.

We shivered, welcoming
   the faint warmth, the shimmering, and then,
      when the sky couldn't hold the sun back any more—
      knife-stab of first ray.

Dawn shone truth from forgery;
      expectation

      dissolved with dawn's mist.
But we'd waited all night for this—light brilliant as fact.
    I let cold light pierce me:

A sunrise is a sadness singed with ecstasy.

sunrise 9

Cows dot the pasture. "We do dot," they'd say if they wanted to argue but had a bad cold.

Cloudy this morning, muted and pale.

sunrise 10

At dawn a reluctance—

My vision is paltry (is faulty); my fingers are slow. There's light, sure, but these deciduous trees are all wintering. And geese—I hear geese outside, honking glory all across the pasture and out toward the faraway pond, geese braving the winter, song-honks interrupting inertia so that it dissipates, drifts.

sunrise 11

I learned early to deal in ideals: certainty, Sunday, silence,
white light, true love, free will, first chair, A-plus, purity, infinity, honors credit, even numbers, whole numbers, right angles,
righteousness, conversion factor, conscience, total immersion,
accuracy, parallel structure, unit circle, noble gases, symmetry,
renunciation, total commitment, proof, evidence, destiny, truth.
Early is on time, and on time is late. Asymptotes reach infinity
finally, and y=mx+b. Preferred symbol: the circle—surpassing
even the cross, which was vertically asymmetrical.
Give me symmetry.
Give me surety.
Get me out
of this cave.

That star-filled night by the river I learned about red shift.
I tensed,
    sensing my own guiding lights shift, drift,
                              edge away.
Void filled the void.
Mud from the river-bank clung to my boots
                       for months.
There are no circles here.
The earth isn't a sphere, or even
a smartly yclept approximation:
not even "oblate
      spheroid."

The North Pole is slightly higher than the average
    surface, the South Pole slightly lower.
There is a depression in the Indian Ocean
    and a lump—*a lump!*—in the Pacific.
The equator itself bulges
      unevenly.

sunrise 12
6:53 A.M. JANUARY 1

I woke at six, but the sun didn't rise fully until around seven,
because it has to come over the mountain.

These are new beginnings, mercies
    new-every-morning,
       coexistent with inescapable
    continuity. We stand both bound
          and unbound by the past. The overlap
            of other dawns,
          other winters,
        wraps its smoky self
          about our ankles,
       or else it embraces us,
     dragging us under,
   dragging us back.
And yet
  we discard whole eternities,
   shrug off whole histories,
    stand here young-dawning and free.

I drove to work through fire-kissed frost.

sunrise 13
6:53 A.M. JANUARY 2

Here barely post-solstice, the colors are muted.
Light seeps through the morning-hung clouds
pretty evenly. This here is the usual: the
morning-gray sky tinting roseward. This isn't:
something's blowing around—It's snow, white
flakes shadowed to flint, silhouetted against
glowing dawn.

sunrise 14
6:53 A.M. JANUARY 3

hope is a most treasured and hammered and dangerous thing

sunrise 15
6:53 A.M. JANUARY 4

There was snow with the sunrise again. Just before the sun rose, a broad ray bolted upward from behind the mountain. The ray was a vertical rainbow, and it lasted on after the sunrise.

sunrise 16
6:53 A.M. JANUARY 5

frosty tangerine

sunrise 17
6:53 A.M. JANUARY 6

eyebrows reaching upward as to grasp a ledge and pull the brain over

sunrise 18
6:53 A.M. JANUARY 7

Does daybreak hurt the horizon? Does it burn.

[I'm awake now—the horizon's fine.]

Everything & everyone with consciousness, please say, "Here." Everything & everyone who feels pain, please say, "Ow." Everything & everyone rejoicing—hey—sing it.

sunrise 19
6:53 A.M. JANUARY 8

I need to see the day breaking—over and over and over again. This is a confrontation, a facing-up to existence itself. I can't confront the whole of existence, not all at once—As Job found, it's too big. But perhaps through a part I can face the whole, looking into its eyes through the dawn every day. "Here I am—and there you are. Well, now."

sunrise 20
6:53 A.M. JANUARY 9

There is a luster, but not yellow or bright. Snow gleams blue, but it isn't a blue that I would want to paint with or wear. The snow isn't new-fallen, either, and I see no moon, only sapphire-cast gunmetal clouds.

sunrise 21
6:53 A.M. JANUARY 10

Avoidance ducks it under—yet attention is buoyant: up and merrily up it comes, bobbing and triumphant.

I know I'll obey, though I hold what I see in abeyance.

The hill is white, and the sky is not as white.

sunrise 22
6:53 A.M. JANUARY 11

Everything and everyone is seeking a place in the story—I've been told.

I may not seek, but if I sit
staunch and dismissive,
I'll be named and cast
into yours. I may dismiss;
   I cannot erase.
Better
to tell a better tale,
spin
a more colorful yarn,
weave a tighter text,
   and wrap you up in it.
Everything without a context
must adopt or be adopted.

sunrise 23
6:53 A.M. JANUARY 12

Mind keeps
  furiously
    calculating
      solutions
        as I sleep,

          then
barrels into philosophical churning the instant I wake.

sunrise 24
6:52 A.M. JANUARY 13

I woke to a tangerine sky, the mountain a
shudder, the rough east gleaming.

sunrise 25
6:52 A.M. JANUARY 14

purple-gray cloud: the mountain lifts a
crooked finger

sunrise 26
6:52 A.M. JANUARY 15

If the sun won't rise visibly anyway,
what's to keep me from facing the west?
This line of persistence may well stand
erect, as a spine.

sunrise 27
6:52 A.M. JANUARY 16

Sunrise and sunset are miniature equinoxes;
midnight and noon tiny solstices.
Miniatures!
Speak,
widen your funnel-mouths;
give up your secrets.
General to specific,
specific to general,
sublime to intimate and back to the sublime.

sunrise 28
6:51 A.M. JANUARY 17

We've got one lens per eye; plenty of creatures
have multiple lenses. The little trilobites and
flies have compound apposition eyes, and they
live in mosaic-worlds. They get kaleidoscope
sunrises. (No. They don't. They have such a
short range of vision that they probably don't.
But many of them can detect polarized light,
and polarization does happen at sunrise. Not as
much as at sunset, but it's there. The critters see
something; they just won't tell us what.)

sunrise 29
6:51 A.M. JANUARY 18

ash-pearl

to golden

(Imagine atoms as tiny tiny pearls, and the whole
world will seem silken.)

sunrise 30
6:51 A.M. JANUARY 19

no subtext without context. all context lost, and sub-text stranded somewhere, mute. now there are sensible boundaries, resounding, sounding off—

"Sound off!"

"Here we are! back behind the mountain! back up to the tree-line! up unto your skin!"

anywhere the light can reach must be safe. there are no sharp corners here, so do not steer as if there were.

sore sore sore sore

(as with a secret)

sunrise 31
6:50 A.M. JANUARY 20

I can do without. Do not try to bring what you cannot give. Live in a light house, and frugally.

sunrise 32
6:50 A.M.   JANUARY 21

old unbroken promises / old and broken promises

sunrise 33
6:49 A.M.   JANUARY 22

The light taps at the back door, delivers a telegram. The sky behind is gray and blank.

sunrise 34
6:49 A.M.   JANUARY 23

The sun is white but shines yellow, because when sunlight hits the atmosphere, it scatters. (Get going.)

The daffodils will be here soon.

sunrise 35

As for #35, what am I to do with a plain gray sky when I just want to sleep? This scene may well be a window to something, but I am not looking very intently. Must I force everything open?

There's nothing happening. Oh, but everything's happening (so I tried to convince or remind myself or you)—We're barreling through space at eighteen-and-a-half miles per second. Is that fast? I can't go a mile in a second, not in my car, anyway. But—the circumference of the earth, at the equator (It's different if you measure through the poles.), is a little over 24,900 miles. The earth's diameter (through the equator again) is 7926.3352 miles.

18.5 miles/second x 60 seconds/minute x 60 minutes/hour x 24 hours/day = 1,598,400 miles/day.

It's not that I am unimpressed. But I'm more impressed with the stillness than with the breakneck speed. (It isn't breaking *my* neck.)

It is a living stillness, like that of my body when I'm resting. My blood flows at about three feet per second when it leaves my heart, slowing down until it reaches the heart again. And I breathe. Keep me perfectly, perfectly still for too long, and I must be permanently excused.

The distance the earth travels in orbit in one day is just 202 times its own diameter. Well, that's rounded up. The calculator says 201.6568787. Pick a day when you don't have to go anywhere much, and don't move any farther than 202 times the thickness of your own body, all day.

sunrise 36
6:48 A.M. JANUARY 25

The point of the sunrise slides
down the mountain
and northward.

Our neighbor
Mr. Mullican
once tried building a pond
in the field, but the ground
wouldn't hold water.
Too porous.

So now
when Mr. Mullican
wants to graze his cattle near a pond,
he uses some other field. Still,

every once in a good rainy while,
the hollowed space fills up again.

Today it holds water,
cups the sun's reflection.

sunrise 37

Stratus clouds, three of them, hover like shielding arms or too-relevant facts. I catch them breaking apart at the top, and I exhale. Now I can take them a little less seriously. Their undersides glow, blushing with sunrise. These are wide clouds; light divulges dimension.

A minute later, the whole sky's a cloud, aflame, and crowding the mountain.

I look again. This is an Escher scene, impossible skies instead of impossible stairs. The sky above the mountain is so smooth and uniform that were it not for those glaucous extensions, left and northward, over the lower, unmountainous treeline, I would perceive the whole upper sky to be clear. Or are those streaks of cloudlessness rather than clouds?

Went to the living room, looked out from there. The sky above the mountain was undoubtedly cloud. But what happened to the stratus? Did it stretch way out, or skedaddle?

Back at my own window, I find the sky cloud-spread:—blue-gray, occasional pink tint, but none of this whole-glowing business. What, all that overture for naught? Day's got to get started. They'll let the sun in the back way today.

sunrise 38
6:46 A.M. JANUARY 27

The flash pond in the field froze before it could take full sleeping leave. Streaks of pink and peach blur, blend; now the pink is spreading like a rash.

As we turn toward the sun, fat packs of rays shoot through the branches of trees on the mountain, so that we see another, erstwhile secret, horizon.

If I'd always been told it, I might well have believed that the sun is a god. I might sing its welcome; I might wonder in dread if it didn't show up straightaway. Yesterday might have unnerved me.

sunrise 39
6:46 A.M. JANUARY 28

A large black spot, like the one in *Treasure Island* but larger, the size of an open hand. It was some kind of black hole that appeared at the end of dreams, and I could go through it if I wanted to keep dreaming. I didn't go through it. I woke, and the morning sky was gray.

sunrise 40
6:45 A.M. JANUARY 29

In light of the sunrise, we're forced into facing our orbit (elliptic).

sunrise 41
6:44 A.M. JANUARY 30

There's snow on the ground. I'm barely
awake. I can hear the geese, somewhere out
in the snow.

sunrise 42
6:44 A.M. JANUARY 31

Just before the sun rose, the eastern sky
turned pink. Below, snow shone dully.
It wasn't luminous—That word's too generous.
Even "blue" is a stretch. It's close to the color
of midday storm clouds gathering, foreboding and thick.
But the snow's form is so foreign the comparison trips.

Once the sun rose, icicles caught the light
and flung it in every direction.
The iced-over maple glimmers
        as if full of spiders' webs.
Yesterday I watched spider webs catch
                        needle-shaped
                            snowflakes.

sunrise 43
6:43 A.M. FEBRUARY 1

Days-old snow covers the ground, and the whole world is buzzing. The snow's only ice now; ice doesn't hush anything.

I am some sorry eye—stuck with specks, blocked with logs!

I thought the sun yesterday would have melted the ice coating the upper branches of those naked, twiggy trees, but the ice is still there, stubborn, thick.

This morning, the clouds were first purple, then cosmetic pink, then that flame-orange, then some kind of yellow, and now that pre-rise pearl-white. Just a few of them, off in the usual direction.

It is six fifty-eight. The clouds are so fulgent that I cannot tell whether or not the sun has yet risen. I don't yet see its delimiting circle. What would we have thought and believed if the sun had no circle, but shone as a larger and amorphous brightness all day?

sunrise 44
6:42 A.M. FEBRUARY 2

snowbones and fog

sunrise 45
6:41 A.M. FEBRUARY 3

When your groggy body says that the world— that most of the world—is irrelevant, listen cautiously.

sunrise 46
6:40 A.M. FEBRUARY 4

A bird lights on the edge of a full five-gallon bucket to drink.

Nearly seven and still no sign of the sun, no sign except the light enough outside; the sun's around here somewhere. Who's been shining on my grass?

If you check the definitions, dawn is when the sky begins to lighten, ending twilight. Sunrise doesn't really happen till the sun itself appears. This is one long dawn.

sunrise 47
6:39 A.M. FEBRUARY 5

When inwardly a vague
dark wave silences
    everything, when silence
itself crashes through, the substance
        which is silence
            demands a confession,
demands some thorny creed,
if only (breakers
    and waves crashing over) "this is it—
this," and "I am undone; I am undone."

sunrise 48
6:39 A.M. FEBRUARY 6

Where is the primal joy and wonder?
Where is the young delight? Are they obscured
    by mere clouds? Are they so easily worn out?
As for the sun, it is missing.
    As for the hill, it's a pale, sickly brown.
Two birdhouses
on two poles:
            watchful.
Every spring
recalls
    other springs,
and every fall
    that fall, and that fall,
            and that fall.
I never get far.

sunrise 49
6:38 A.M. FEBRUARY 7

Minutes too early for sunrise, we're riding
out the dawn. The sky's a soft gray, a muted
raspberry flame way yonder on back. The
clouds clump, thick as yogurt.

A murmuration of starlings rattles like a tambourine.

Deciduous branches part sky.

sunrise 50
6:37 A.M. FEBRUARY 8

"They are new every morning"—and what if the past six mornings were gray? Is there yet a newness to come? There could well be newer, stranger newnesses, lurking somewhere still-hidden.

Blue clouds have come in now to smother the blush. The craggy old pear tree stands black against blue.

sunrise 51
6:36 A.M. FEBRUARY 9

A she-cardinal surveys the morning, moving jerkily. The birds are strong enough to stand in such breezes. A wind's stirring everything up. It sounds a low wheeze, long tones blown on a lone glass bottle.

The near trees are shaking; the farther ones stand unaffected and still.

sunrise 52
6:35 A.M. FEBRUARY 10

I won't bombard you. There isn't the time. My hands are washed clean, lightly floured, well-practiced, and I will not hand you what you do not actually need.

sunrise 53
6:34 A.M. FEBRUARY 11

One bright and bleeding mandarin smashes against the blue mountain and cloud.

Oh, world! You tempt me! (To what? To watch? Then please keep at it—I keep my working eyes closed far too much of the time.)

Four birds roost in the maple tree—five—six, seven.

The U. S. Naval Observatory's data says that the sunrise was at 6:34 today. I timed it at 6:48; that's over the low end of the mountain. And at 6:49, the sun threw a leg up over the mountain, a slender crescent of light spilling over. If you pick at a straight edge of paper, like a page in a book, you can crease out a small slender crescent like this.

sunrise 54
6:33 A.M. FEBRUARY 12

Uncivil twilight? It was civil enough to me.

And later, out in the cold open square, one metallic click resounded (coffee cup / coat button).

sunrise 55
6:32 A.M. FEBRUARY 13

I have seen this day before.
I have seen this day begin before.
I have written words like these before.
Endless variation or
none? Potentially
endless variation within
tight tight constrictions.
A mathematician might meet
better success. Or
am I stuck with
questions math
won't answer?

want: drift,
   anonymity,
       to disappear,
    to reappear,
          to reminisce,
     to know,
       to be re-known;
       renown?
  bad limbo to live in

the days aren't endless and you've got to build them into
something

sunrise 56
6:31 A.M. FEBRUARY 14

Suddenly everything is steeped in terms of survival.

I underestimate plenty.

Now, morning dawns all around in the hidden surrounding
horizons. Day breaks under bushes and into the still violet
in-between-everything air. I hear a meadowlark.

sunrise 57
6:30 A.M. FEBRUARY 15

Light woke me.

Snow, drifting: sky, calm.

It's rising fast fast fast so bright I can't look out the window!

Keep to the shadows; they are just blue enough to be safe.

The shadows are angled. The snow at its brightest is only more sunlight, ornery, white, and fierce.

Those flakes that fell sometime last night are out there reflecting and melting, melting and reflecting and stretching and melting.

sunrise 58
6:28 A.M. FEBRUARY 16

The sun rises early (because of refraction); (because of the distance) the sun rises late.

sunrise 59
6:27 A.M. FEBRUARY 17

A patchy yard is disappointing if you don't want to see the snow melt; a patchy sky would have been colorful.

sunrise 60
6:26 A.M. FEBRUARY 18

Those tiny snowcapped mountains in the yard
    are just bunches of monkey-grass,
standing bold to catch the snow,
    spreading wide their narrow hands,
and look where it got them.

As for the horizon:
    the sun has covered a great distance
northward already, just since the solstice.

Sky: perfectly clear.

Two rays appear
    like two piercing eyes, shining
through the trees at the base of the mountain,
    before the light bridges the treeline.

Those two hiked, got here early.
And there
    is the whole fiery circle!
Not a bit of it's yet past the treeline.

Once the sun rose
over that second and scraggly horizon,
    to the left of it hovered
    a small extra circle of light.

sunrise 61
6:25 A.M. FEBRUARY 19

Frost and then the shy horizon—
   The morning was brighter
twenty minutes ago. Why's it fading,
     now that we're nearer the sun? Come,
        let's have some colors;
       let's have a song to sing down the night.

Just above the timberline, a small bright-orange smudge,
     like a smeared thumbprint.
        Is that our prelude?

There is the sun—Will it be enough to warm me?

I want to inhale life and light
  at some somehow-perfect angle.
There is usually more good than I raise my eyes to meet;
    real and lasting good requires sacrifice
   and more effort than I initially want to offer;
and nothing can be recaptured.

sunrise 62
6:24 A.M. FEBRUARY 20

Give me a bright penny to lure me out of this
sleep!

The light pushes its way through the woods.
Like a ball of red clay pushed through a
grater, then mashed back together again, the
sun pieces itself back together here west of
the treeline.

sunrise 63
6:23 A.M. FEBRUARY 21

Frost covers the ground, even though yesterday was warm. I don't see any clouds, but there are contrails (I don't count them as clouds.), mostly headed north and west. They tear out across the horizon, and the people up there are watching the sun rise from some crazy angle, drinking coffee and ginger ale, reading or praying or trying to sleep.

The contrails spread out and become clouds—count as clouds—soon enough. I give up and grant them amnesty. The sun isn't up yet, but the contrails-counted-clouds are so bright that I can barely look. One ray pierces the woods. Before the real sun, a fulgid, round, heralding cloud forms just above the lone ray, so bright it erases a whole inch of the treeline. (The light caught in my eyes blurs this ink as I write.)

The heralding cloud rises—It is the real sun! The ray in the woods is the extra, the ghost, the understudy, the shadow. Jealous understudy to the sun.

sunrise 64
6:22 A.M. FEBRUARY 22

And what do I need? To be shot through: to be shot through with light.

sunrise 65
6:20 A.M. FEBRUARY 23

Truth lies there on the kitchen table, to the left of the car keys, waiting for the coffee.

(Tell me the truth doesn't lie.)

Find where the truth lies, and where joy resides, and "offer your bodies as a living sacrifice" / "for our God is a consuming fire."

sunrise 66
6:19 A.M. FEBRUARY 24

one long, slow, cool, blue dawn

sunrise 67
6:18 A.M. FEBRUARY 25

The sun rose clean, silent and hidden. The sky pales; light seeps in, slips in the back door.

Balance: equilibrium. Osmosis involves a lightness, an openness, and a (certain) hardening.

sunrise 68
6:17 A.M. FEBRUARY 26

O! and I woke to a day and a darling! and O!
It is more than I expected! and O! I am too
easily affected!

sunrise 69
6:15 A.M. FEBRUARY 27

This dawn has no rosy fingers. She lost them
in a fight, else they froze in the frost and fell
off. She has only the one great, cold, bald
head, which lifts itself slowly, wearily.
Winter-dull olive rises from beneath the fading frost. I'm watching for where secrets rise:
They rise unbidden. I do not want to say
where they've been hidden.

sunrise 70
6:14 A.M. FEBRUARY 28

This morning it suddenly struck me as very
funny that phones vibrate. Especially if you
think of them as hedgehogs.

sunrise 71
6:13 A.M. MARCH I

O, and the streak of the butter along the broad breadbun. O, and the streak of the steam-trails through rosy-glow dawn.

sunrise 72
6:11 A.M. MARCH 2

Now that the sun is well-risen, what is this "can't move on"? The world will move you on. The train must depart; if you're on it, you're taking off, too. "All aboard!" Do you want to stand here, stranded, gawking at the station? Its walls and columns are fashioned of marble from the famed pre-war cathedral, but you've other cities to visit.

Ration the mornings gingerly as you will, one day the cupboard will be empty, and though you wind the dear clock, it will not run. So pray, yes, do pray, but mean it. Do you know what you want?

sunrise 73
6:10 A.M. MARCH 3

Sky's gray.

What is this—this hunger
unrelenting? A fear of missing
the one scene on which hinges
the rest of the plot?
The wan curiosity of orbit,
the gravitational need
for the center? The need
to face one's torturer
or only love?

Sunrise, cloud-shrouded,
doesn't dazzle
like stars, does not
enchant (or quench
thirst) like the moon,
but confronts,
              enlivens.
Stars call forth
involuntary regard;
sunrise commands it,
    or else
asks directly.

And the young day breaks.

sunrise 74
6:09 A.M. MARCH 4

Clouds spread to catch
the young day's light and split it
        into colors.
Clouds billow without
smothering the sun
or softening the silhouettes.

6:14 a.m.—their undersides glow orange and coral.

Sweet sun, come rising over there, through the forest-
ed thicket and over the mountain behind. The sun's
fuzzy for obstructions, bright as an epiphany, smooth
as naked grape—its circle fully visible before it's past
the treeline.

6:24 a.m.—meadowlark

sunrise 75
6:07 A.M. MARCH 5

Our airy atmospheric
periscope forecasts the future,
telegraphs the fiery good news.
Light bends across the horizon and shows us
      the sun
before we can see it from naked planet and with naked eyes.

Sweet east, bring us day again.

Day, break open
      your eastern horizon, show us
your secrets. Don't think we won't tell them; they beg
      to be spread.

sunrise 76
6:06 A.M. MARCH 6

This is the scene: We are facing the east. We face a wire fence and a pasture.

Stage right: the indigo mountain, which climbs up and off to the south.

Stage left: pasture, trees, mere horizon, and sometimes the lights of the town.

Dawn: cloud-muted, post-rain.

sunrise 77
6:05 A.M. MARCH 7

The still-bare black trees, vertical lines, stand perpendicular to swaths of orange and blue.

6:20 a.m.—The sun's already up: it is that bright smudge behind the translucence.

sunrise 78
6:03 A.M. MARCH 8

One cloud veils the sky. The veil bears tiny scattered shining breaks, four worn-out places in the fabric. As day gains, the sun—seen or no—burns through the worn weave of the everyday, workaday cloth. We've reached a thin place—Come, stand in it.

The lustrous cloud fragmented (catching and refracting precious light) a mountain's height above the mountain.

sunrise 79
6:02 A.M. MARCH 9

Before sunrise: the eastern sky glowed, a hot iron.

After: quick and silver bird wings.

sunrise 80
6:01 A.M. MARCH 10

secretive east

sunrise 81
5:59 A.M. MARCH 11

one smudge of a blush

and the grass is growing: onions first.

sunrise 82
5:58 A.M. MARCH 12

Not yet six and already red: all right. I've been
warned. East's pink was brief, smothered within
minutes by soft deceptive blue.

sunrise 83
5:56 A.M. MARCH 13

Hold it steady, everybody, we'll all turn toward the light—We'll catch the light and carry it all day. In the morning your skin will tell stories; your hair will smell like campfire. The light will come on in, even through clouds—It may not be yellow and it may not be warm, but as light is light, it warms you; this is all you will need.

sunrise 84
6:55 A.M. MARCH 14

Trade an hour for the light if that is what you like: shine, shine, and spend it.

And what are you doing with circles? Amorously, feverishly, furiously calculating. This interrogation may well tell you more and more of what you want to know—never all. The secret is too lengthy, precise, and fine: Your ears are far too dull. You will give up on listening, or else you'll die straining to hear.

sunrise 85
6:54 A.M. MARCH 15

The time change means that the sun rises later—what was six is now seven—and I gain an hour of sleep.

sunrise 86
6:52 A.M. MARCH 16

Birdsongs are rising. The morning's overcast; the sun won't even pick a spot on the horizon. Birdsongs are rising, though—purple martin, chickadee!

sunrise 87
6:51 A.M. MARCH 17

Obstinate gray.

I could find the sunrise in birds' songs (A doubter might find faith within his doubt.)—The birds are explaining, explaining, explaining—The song shifts now, changes shape; now it's spreading.

Spring is on its way; the vernal equinox will be here soon. I'll take an equinox; I'll eat it with a spoon.

sunrise 88
6:49 A.M. MARCH 18

slow-flickering dawn

You know and I know full well I'm not telling you the whole story. I couldn't if I wanted to—and you, were you telling, you wouldn't tell all, even if you could.

I didn't know until this year how often clouds simply smother the fun.

sunrise 89
6:48 A.M. MARCH 19

Morning broke like an egg, sudden with colors and light and all you could want or expect.

One star shone back at the sun from atop the wet fencepost. The rain on the fencepost reflected: so it was a moon. Moons orbit; I'm orbiting—I can't get away.

sunrise 90
6:46 A.M. MARCH 20

Overnight and out of town. "You won't be able to see," she warned, and I wasn't. The light I saw wasn't the sun—more eager than keen, I gasped, but "it's just a security light." I wrapped up, tried the door—tried the other door, stepped outside, out into urban buzzing, a colossal mechanical drone. Birds keep singing, furiously.

Equatorial, precarious—as at the solstice, I half-believe or imagine I feel some kind of balance. Through the cloud of such roaring small sound, I welcome the sun, welcome the lumbering train.

The morning, the city, the world—all are already teeming. There will be no silence today.

sunrise 91
6:45 A.M.   MARCH 21

I turned to see the sun, such a red-orange I stood rapt, rising two-thirds the way up the south side of the old green hill. Already down from the mountain, it slid further north up the hill, behind the gray curtains all those cloudy mornings.

Up a full three minutes, bright and a very red, and as it rose it disappeared again.

Now at 7:22, it's high, high, high and up again, out again, the golden sort of white out sweet against the pale cloudy blue.

sunrise 92
6:44 A.M.   MARCH 22

The earth waits.

The chloroplasts are waiting. Plants everywhere are holding their water and carbon dioxide, waiting for the energy to turn it into oxygen and sugar. Flowers wait on the day-flying insects to come in, poke around, fly away, pollinate. The diurnal lizards are waiting. We're waiting.

If all these chemicals, these atoms of all these molecules, were rearranged so that our bodies were not our bodies and we couldn't live here, and neither could any birds, and this rock we call our whole world was no more than rock and strange gases, nothing about it would be disappointed a bit if for some reason it hurtled out of its orbit forever or for moments.

Fair far exogenous fire—come!

sunrise 93
6:42 A.M. MARCH 23

"Stream-of-consciousness is our only hope."

Barely coherent at sunrise. The stream itself
is our chief hope. A consciousness beyond
my own is my only hope. The hope is to get
somewhere, to go somewhere—whether we
go of ourselves or are carried.

Solipsism won't do it. I need a real foothold.

The longer those trees stand, the more they
can tell—but trees don't tell secrets to me.
They only tell what they tell everyone,
through their textures, through their shapes.

sunrise 94
6:41 A.M. MARCH 24

Mist hung over hill and field.
   A round scoop
of orange juice concentrate
   rose, with healing in its wings,
a shadow at the base
   of every
blade of grass.

sunrise 95
6:39 A.M. MARCH 25

"Morning brings back the heroic ages,"
Thoreau said. Cloud mornings, too, Henry
David? Thunderstorms inspire—but clouds
enervated as these?

sunrise 96
6:38 A.M. MARCH 26

Before pale light spread, the morning's
clouds gathered brooding and monstrous—
fists rather than water or paper.

sunrise 97
6:36 A.M. MARCH 27

Dip a crisp blue sky a wafer into milky light.

Rise behind the maple tree and hide until
you cannot hide, until there is nothing left to
hide. Bake a dawn all day.

Luminescent daffodils shine light-thirsty yellow.

sunrise 98
6:35 A.M.   MARCH 28

Last night I left the window open
to the storm. I slept so sound
I woke well before the alarm,
woke to rainfall.
The sun didn't rise; we rose
toward the light through the thundering
    rain.

At eight o'clock, from behind the closed blinds
shone a bright clean-angled square of light.
I pulled the string, unclosed the blinds—
now I'm unblinded, and
      blinded.

sunrise 99
6:34 A.M.   MARCH 29

Day unfolds, the silver light explaining
everything.

"I shall know why—when Time is
over—," Emily Dickinson wrote, looking for Christ then to "explain each
separate anguish / In the fair school-
room of the sky—." Today we see each
separate blade of grass; our anguishes
are not explained. The what, perhaps
(more than we may want to know),
never that cagey kernel of why.

sunrise 100
6:32 A.M. MARCH 30

Above the mist-hung meadow, the sky's
clear: palest peach fades upward to blue.
6:41 and we've got it—coming up over the
hill. Still gelatinous, as it's been so many
mornings lately, a glistening orange gelatin
sherbet. It's plasma. It's got enough ionized
particles to count, and a mass great enough
that it holds itself together pretty well. But
without that great gravity, the plasma (Solar
wind is plasma; and plasma fills the space
between the planets, the space between the
star systems, the space between the galaxies.)
wouldn't have any definite shape. I could
spoon a scoop or two into a dish, and the
sunstuff would spread out to fit. And it
would spill over the top, unless we had a lid.
It might not be so nice to eat.

sunrise 101
6:31 A.M. MARCH 31

moonset in the west against a flat and
periwinkle sky

sunrise 102
6:29 A.M. APRIL I

No tricks here: the air is clear, its clarity definite, prominent.

No tricks: But I don't see the world as it is. Birds see ultraviolet light, which is invisible to me. My own perception deceives me, but I haven't dismissed it yet. The data's transformed, converted, translated, and we know all we need to survive, yes? But we none of us survive, and the translators are traitors.

I woke, slept, woke to the alarm and to light reflected off the cover of the book beside me. The ripened east has reached ochre; mares' tails swirl white above. The row of trees thins at the top of the hill. The sun's rising there now, burning its way through the trees.

Welcome: bright sky quivering just before the sun shows. A thin cloud disperses the light of the sun, already risen. It's 6:38.

sunrise 103

All's brighter sooner
these days. Slow to happen,
but I am slower to take note.
    At sunrise,
fire-colors catch fast,
    shine vibrantly.
        They vibrate,
    peak to trough to peak,
        so we can see.
    "So," indeed.
We're hit with wavelengths
skies and grasses wouldn't
        swallow. More than a matter
of color, these grasses
    are hungry.
They print their own energy
        currency.
    Let them eat
        adenosine triphosphate;
    let them eat sugar.
The dew doesn't blanket; it illuminates.
        Before the sun has even
    risen, the eastern
landscape is all light and silhouette
        and wet and eager green.

sunrise 104
6:26 A.M. APRIL 3

The morning is cool, not golden, though fair. From inside I could hear the birds more clearly than the traffic. I've picked out at least six birds, six songs—There are more, but their voices are tangled; I've lost track.

Out east, to my left, stretches one long diagonal streak of slate cloud; furthest east, smudge of peach.

Breezes wrap around me, and I shiver, though I'm wrapped up in a shawl. No cold reaches my feet, bare on this wooden deck.

Stepped back inside. Seven years ago—even five—I was a more passionate, more strident romantic. How can I yearn to be free and yet want to be encased, enclosed, enveloped? Once inside, I want the breezes again—clement, slight, wild as flowers.

Back upstairs, I eased the window loose. Before my grip was strong enough to hoist it up an inch, I raised it a *crack*, and against it, wind moaned; the wind had cause to moan.

sunrise 105
6:25 A.M. APRIL 4

unmerciful to the possibility / merciful to the possibility

sunrise 106
6:24 A.M. APRIL 5

The fact of unmistakably grows brighter, stronger every day. You already know better than I do it's spring. Equinox, daffodils, sun, Easter, dew. It's hot in some places. The pear tree's in full bloom. Verdure is taking the mountain, advancing upward and fast— winter, trapped at the peak, has nowhere to go. We'll see it fall soon.

sunrise 107
6:22 A.M. APRIL 6

Pines sway beneath the waning half-moon to the south. East, crazed carrot-lit contrails bring desperate plane crashes to mind, but only the wind did the twisting.

sunrise 108
6:21 A.M. APRIL 7

The sky burned early, then faded to soft streaks of copper, pink, and pale purple, cerulean above all. Something small and blank and frightening: the chill is real. Obligation to love everything? It will break any of us.

sunrise 109
6:20 A.M. APRIL 8

vast, fast rain; day rising and everything green

sunrise 110
6:18 A.M. APRIL 9

The youngly green leaves of the maple tree, innocent, have taken on a reddish tint, here in this dawn-light and against the ice, the light frost that settled last night. "We loiter in winter while it is already spring," Thoreau wrote, calling me out. Spring creeps in beneath our feet, slides in beneath, then acts as a lever to lift us. But, hear! Hear, Thoreau— winter won't be shaken so easily. Our senses are dulled, brains frozen for months, and just as we're thawing, a frost bites again. The world wants to go back to sleep. It won't. But waking, as birth or as hemisphere-wide thaw and blossoming, is its own struggle, if not epic, then memorable, your "memorable crisis which all things proclaim."

6:21—The leaves are green against the bright orange rising sun, green again against the ice.

sunrise 111
6:17 A.M. APRIL 10

Now that the maple tree has met spring, the sun has an extra forest to rise behind and through. The tree's long, leafy arm extends over and before the far line of trees, which rim the green hill like thinning, unkempt, wiry hair.

These colors are strange and arresting—like yesterday's, what with the frost. Not until frost is no longer a given do I think anything of it. The natural climate patterns here jolt me into curiosity. There's more I'd ask, if I tried, or if I let another place jolt me: the givens here aren't givens everywhere.

Frost grows; frost does not fall. Frost grows right up from the surfaces of things colder than the surrounding air—and grass, bless it, does get that cold. Frost grows up in spicules, which are tiny spikes.

I'd thought there might be a name for the frosts that fall, that *grow*—after the year has warmed to welcome mere dew again. *The Farmer's Almanac* carries old names for each month's full moon: April's is the Pink Moon. There are no such names for frosts. Not around here. We only want to know when they'll go, not to return until fall.

sunrise 112
6:15 A.M. APRIL 11

What happened this morning? I am not quite sure. Time was running out, and the voices were performing violent acrobatics in the predawn morning air.

sunrise 113
6:14 A.M. APRIL 12

This is a dawn all green and gold, with deep jade shadows in the grasses. One far tree stretches a wire fence taut from two directions: a right angle. Its new-grown leaves spread to catch the light; the surrounding trees are all shadow.

sunrise 114
6:13 A.M. APRIL 13

This glossary of astronomical terms contains fossils of a worldview long discarded. "Sunrise" is a common fossil, but it's not the only one. The "ecliptic" is "the apparent path of the Sun along the celestial sphere." In the *Almagest*, Ptolemy's, the ecliptic is the actual path of the sun—the sun, of course, orbiting the earth.

For Ptolemy, astronomy was more than the mere measuring of the natural world. This theoretical discipline was closely linked to theology, concerned with "divine and heavenly things"—the movements of heavenly beings. Astronomy could "prepare understanding persons with respect to nobleness of actions and character by means of the sameness, good order, due proportion, and simple directness contemplated in divine things, making its followers lovers of that divine beauty, and making habitual in them, and as it were natural, a like condition of the soul."

If Ptolemy could have learned that the universe is asymmetrical, would he have proclaimed divine beauty to be the same?

sunrise 115
6:11 A.M.   APRIL 14

Any man who dares to change the language will for some time be misunderstood.

There exists a necessary darkness. Shadows in the pine trees are the quietest. The hair of the black cat glints gold; triangles of light flash from black birds' wings. The mist out south is soft, cool blue; the cloud in the north field glows pink. As the sun rises, the shadows of small things grow darker and more sharply defined.

This any heart may own, if only heart will grow to own it.

sunrise 116
6:10 A.M.   APRIL 15

Austere dawn: back in the dark, before and behind this fearsome young morning, lie promises we made while dawning.

sunrise 117
6:09 A.M.   APRIL 16

At the helm and in the belly of this hunger to see is a corresponding hunger to be seen. *When shall I come and appear before my God.* The green-grown trees stand taller and closer together now, grown out of the bare bark of winter. The dew shines white; the sun rises red. I watch its bold rays; ignited, I open.

sunrise 118
6:07 A.M.   APRIL 17

The gray sky's arrested by the steady strides of a strong, deliberate green. I am fastened to a self, to need for sleep, to day; the day is fastened to a little box beside a stapled sheaf of paper.

I reach for the stapler and staple myself and the day to finitude, to hope, and to morrow. The puncture wounds resulting are canals that irrigate the days and stapled papers with the waters of infinity.

sunrise 119
6:06 A.M.   APRIL 18

The sun's rising redder: no more the bold, cold, yellow direct. This is a setting sun rising. We don't normally see such a high concentration of particles in the air until the evening—They've been blowing around all day; they need night to settle them down. Is this pollen, or volcanic ash?

Minutes pass. Dark, exuberant billows rise from the northeast; the sun glints as flame in the dewy brown grass.

sunrise 120
6:05 A.M.   APRIL 19

how the upper dome cupped us so perfectly blue down unto confusion (cloud boundary—defining, disorients) above and behind all the summering, stubborn deep green

sunrise 121
6:04 A.M.   APRIL 20

Bare feet firmly in the cold
wet grass, I can't call the blue
unearthly. "Luminous" would overdo;
we've all overdone enough.
This here outdoes me.
All that's not dawn-aching sky
swells, shows all its blue.

sunrise 122
6:02 A.M.   APRIL 21

The pain upon waking was jarring. If I kept
the sun in a jar I would open it every morning.

The mist, thick, glows. Essences (such as
that color) drift up expectantly, offering
themselves for perception—for codification,
canonization, imprisonment, sweet recognition.

sunrise 123
6:01 A.M.   APRIL 22

I looked up, and the first ray shone plain,
bright and direct through far idle indigo
clouds and the trees, not heeding the pal-
isade entranceway so many cumulus, high-
piled and fantastic, had so effusively laid out
for it.

sunrise 124
6:00 A.M.   APRIL 23

Horizon can only promise you what it can honestly offer: a circle about you, circumscribed to break and to steady your view.

sunrise 125
5:59 A.M.   APRIL 24

The question of whether is only a question of when. A question of weather forever, a question of whether we'll win. A question of winning forever or never: baste fabric or turkey. A question of whether's a question of yearning.

sunrise 126
5:58 A.M.   APRIL 25

Yes to bare feet; it is April. And yes to any illuminative stab at all the roiling black out back.

At twilight, darkness and light brush past one another. Civil or uncivil, you ask? Both—and always silent. An unspoken "Ah—there you are," exulting or grim, at each passing, each change of the guard. Day breaks, or night falls, and there's no snapping string, no shattering glass, no jagged pieces to sweep up or tiptoe around. A brief encounter, a hard stare or a furtive embrace, and then a clean break, clean unless you count shadows, dark closets, the moon.

sunrise 127
5:56 A.M. APRIL 26

Waking early can be
a brief break

in the darkness,
when air, combating gravity
to orbit
an ideal (a far yet constant
source of light),
pushes upward
from within.

Sunrise, illuminating,
affirms—repudiates.
No: start over.
Try writing left-handed.
Change angles.

Volition looms lit and insoluble.

sunrise 128
5:55 A.M. APRIL 27

with silence (and trills, calls, and oneupbirdship)

sunrise 129
5:54 A.M. APRIL 28

Likelihood is hardly a concern. At six, the day is
emerging, and creeping, creeping out alive.

sunrise 130

5:53 A.M. APRIL 29

The fields are white but not ready for harvest. So what are they white unto? They're white with rime, or else with mist or reason. The mist surrenders, letting risen day lift it. The fields are white unto surrendering. And are they white unto a lie? They're white unto winter, and hiding, and finding themselves now forbidden to hide.

sunrise 131

5:52 A.M. APRIL 30

The sun's rays shoot through the woods, and they make it out quivering. The fingers strain to the tops of the trees, and the sun comes climbing on over.

sunrise 132

5:51 A.M. MAY I

There wasn't a sunrise; thunder rolled me, rolled through everything, rolled and rolled on. Severe-weather sirens pollute storms.

sunrise 133
5:50 A.M. MAY 2

was wet, wet beyond repeating window
panes, beating loud and round, while light
softened, diluted.

A punctiliar sense of total thankfulness
stretches to reach all the stars, all angling
meteor streaks and illumined moons and
down into every gray everyday bucket.

sunrise 134
5:49 A.M. MAY 3

Here, I will hand you a dish, averring, if you
aren't so averse.

Bread? Light? I tell you, it is sweet. Here,
taste and see.

sunrise 135
5:48 A.M. MAY 4

A lavender sky looms over a lake. The half-
moon's still out. Twilight retreats east, af-
fronted by the garish green of grass trapped
under artificial light.

At six, through the mist, a red fox.

sunrise 136
5:47 A.M. MAY 5

4:50 a.m.—I haven't slept at all. The moon's shone alabaster all night. Darkness is receding. Low east—behind the dark trees and low to the horizon—is already showing some pink. The thumbnail moon's still out, yellower than earlier. There are still stars. If they spin out of control, I'll be awake for it.

sunrise 137
5:46 A.M. MAY 6

Dawn is a soft, weighted, faultless hello (the way-crossing you both could feel coming) from over great distance. At noon, we're miles closer, with all secrets told. No one looks straight into the thing so forbiddingly fiery and high; no one whispers.

sunrise 138
5:45 A.M. MAY 7

No such sunrise. No such fox. No such coffee, and no colors—the *clouds* are rising, actually, and voices from the kitchen.

sunrise 139
5:44 A.M. MAY 8

I pace barefoot outside, so to seal with cold dew a truce with waking reality.

I layered up before climbing on out. The sun's rising now, over a low row of blue clouds. Another, higher cloud row splits the light into upstreaming rays.

The dream existed in my mind and body alone. This grass is cold. The early air is cold and clear.

sunrise 140
5:43 A.M. MAY 9

green and orange and horizontal

sunrise 141
5:42 A.M. MAY 10

The maple tree and all the farther-back trees of its cohort are sifting the sun into crumbs. Now out from under the arm of the tree comes the sun.

Roll out your own carpet of light. I'm closing the window again.

sunrise 142
5:41 A.M. MAY 11

The sun is rising with a vengeance: a vengeance it's got to be, through all this wind, or else a hard, even intention to rescue.

Suppose the sun is sentient: it feels the magnificent force of its own gravitational pull; it wants everything (or pulls like it does, even if it doesn't); it knows better than we do the hot fury of its interior and its surface.

The light shines in the darkness, and the darkness does not comprehend it.

sunrise 143
5:40 A.M. MAY 12

One cow is reflecting the sun off its right side as if it were a white car and not a white cow.

sunrise 144
5:39 A.M. MAY 13

The chill comes in to startle you awake and warn you back to sleep. The chill comes in to startle you awake and into hiding.

sunrise 145
5:39 A.M. MAY 14

Open windows, eyes, blinds, stomata. Rise to remember what could be forgotten, and water it.

sunrise 146
5:38 A.M. MAY 15

One swath of the still sky is lavender. Geese from the far pond, far because we cannot see it from here, bellow, air pumping from the goose abdomen, out the goose throat. I hear the far traffic—far because its roaring is muted by damp air and by its own sparsity. Each standing thing, entering light, gains its own shadow.

sunrise 147
5:37 A.M. MAY 16

It's past eight now, and raining.

I'm behind the times, a whole season behind. Here at mid-May, these full verdant mornings still stand as exception to so many bare winter dawns; life insists upon itself, and the greens deepen.

sunrise 148
5:36 A.M. MAY 17

It's cloudy out, but "gray" won't suffice; there's blue enough in all that's living verdigris; there's life and light enough. I would say the morning is slumbering, but for the meadowlark; minutes later, the mockingbird.

sunrise 149
5:36 A.M. MAY 18

The first ray reflects from the underbelly of a plane headed east. Because of the rounded horizon and corresponding atmosphere, the plane appears to be flying almost straight down—east and south. Branches split the sun, the light, mosaically.

sunrise 150
5:35 A.M. MAY 19

I can distinguish among the birds' voices. I'm pleased; a few days ago, I couldn't tell you when one stopped singing and another took over. These birds of different species can't be ignoring each other. They might be trying. But they may well be arguing over what the dawn is, how its light is best translated into song.

Pale xanthous spots, star-sized, appear in the trees to the east.

Those rays seem to part their surroundings, as fire through cloth or as hikers' hacking hands through thorny undergrowth.

sunrise 151
5:34 A.M. MAY 20

Once the light breaks, but before the light rises, dawn is a gong, or else dawn is a long pianissimo timpani roll.

Birds secure their improbable perches.

sunrise 152
5:34 A.M. MAY 21

Clouds gather the mountains. Unblown petunias slant east. The dog heaves, rhythmically.

sunrise 153
5:33 A.M. MAY 22

One dry maple helicopter stands at a slant, supported by the grasp of the earth. The hub is stuck safe in a tangle of a little bit of everything; the blade balances, resting on air.

The blade jerks.

It twisted, as a key twists in a keyhole, then returned to its original position with a sudden and musical motion. I stared. I waited, and after a pause, the key twisted again. Another long pause—another quick twist. And so on.

Maple seeds autorotate on their way down, to drill themselves into the ground. But the rest of the dry seeds right here, having landed, are still. Have I caught this maple seed in the act of settling in, hanging the upholstery, painting the trim? Or is it some ground-dwelling insect's showy swinging door?

The starlings are loudest this morning. We're off to a cloudy start.

sunrise 154
5:32 A.M.   MAY 23

Distance lolls about as fog between observer and observed. The morning's early fog lies thick and high. The old pear tree and the lone cherry are a deep amethyst-green.

Everybody stretch your arms out! Make sure you can't touch anyone! We don't mind the spaces between and among us; except for hunger, we keep well content.

Looking over my shoulder on my way to check the cherry trees, I see the rising sun, arcing south as I cross the yard. The sun and I stride past a distant row of trees and meet at a clearing, where I turn away.

The sun floods the mist gold, and I go back to bed with grass on my feet.

sunrise 155
5:32 A.M.   MAY 24

The fog languishes, amid trills. The thing to chase away is the darkness. The thing to keep chasing is darkness.

sunrise 156
5:31 A.M. MAY 25

The black wings of those fat gobbling birds
      slice the light.
Wings can't stay black and do that:
      dark silver triangles flash
just above the fencepost, flash against the grass.

I yawn, emerging from the morning's golden green
      ensconcing sepals.

sunrise 157
5:31 A.M. MAY 26

As the sun rose, even the trees shone metallic.

Some cherries have ripened. Some, on the south-
west side of the tree, I still can't see well enough
to tell. They're still submerged in a shadow—
which isn't a shadow proper, but a light that
ought to have a taste.

sunrise 158
5:30 A.M. MAY 27

Mist, lit: thickest I've seen.
    I fell back
      into a winding
  and necessary dream.
The cherries stayed
    to ripen
    until noon
  or to feed
    greedy birds.

sunrise 159
5:30 A.M. MAY 28

After the sun had risen and before the dew
had burned away, a flock of starlings rose
and settled, rose and settled, circling. They
rose in fans and settled in showers. Their
tapering wings caught the radiance as it
shot down from the sun and up-reflected
from the still-dew-laced field. The flock rattled, visually, like the mail-bedecked circumference of a tambourine.

sunrise 160
5:29 A.M. MAY 29

I learn of Saint Brigid, of Celtic and Cath-
olic tradition, born at sunrise, as her moth-
er stepped over a threshold. How like a
sunrise at birth? I wonder. If ever the hour
arrives, I'll listen for sunrise. Patches of
sunlight fall on the field like blood or like
cries.

sunrise 161
5:29 A.M. MAY 30

I had to go to the graveyard just to see anything. The woodthrush varied its song,
sang staccato.

Endeavor to shiver: hold still. Shudders
devour what's useless. Maybe the cold will
jolt the heart back into action.

There are the mosquitoes, a small cloud
buzzing; there are the geese.

Birds sing water-weighted songs. The grass
in the pasture glows rosy.

sunrise 162
5:29 A.M. MAY 31

We drifted in as on a tide, in waves,
        as onto a wet shifting shore.
Dawn: a fine point of precedence.
        Day eased in through rain, steady
                and insisting.
Concede me something: anything
        makes a fair decent story if
                it happened
        at some faraway train station.
Clouds dull the light;
                the green and non-green
        things sort out the remaining ·
                frequencies.

sunrise 163

there's a bird with a chirp like a tink
tink banging on a plate.

black umbrellas stand in the still-muted
light. the cats were all winding away,
away, as salmon upstream or as eels
across meadows or as children en-
tranced following the pied piper.

there was a latch on the door in the
corner of the yard. I had to latch it shut
before I came inside. the short curved
sections of the winding short fencing
(through grass, over hills, through high
grass) of the fenced-in winding way all
the cats in the world trailed along, me-
owing and growling and yowling—they
had latches, too. once I found them, I
unhinged so many hinges, and then the
cats were free.

the screen door cut up the light into a
grid of blinking squares.

this was all hours before the light
reached the roofs of the big black umbrellas. then there at the end, a bird
with a chirp like a bang on a plate.
tink tink tink

sunrise 164
5:28 A.M. JUNE 2

Sometimes this black cat hunkers down, and he looks like an animal I do not know, his head thrust forward, his neck parallel to the ground.

I believe that is the sun, back there so low in the woods. It is either that or a golden calf. The rays are not penetrating, but they are present, and therefore penetrating. The light stands so low in the forest—diffused, the light that escaped panting, refugee light. It stands, self-possessed, owning the wood and owning the world.

It is either the sun, or it is a golden calf, but if it is a calf, its feet are not touching the ground.

sunrise 165
5:28 A.M. JUNE 3

East, I have you.

sunrise 166
5:30 A.M. JUNE 4

East! I must have you.

sunrise 167
5:30 A.M. JUNE 5

"Ol' deadheads," Mrs. Mary used to say while pruning these petunias, scolding the blossoms for drying up, wasting good petunia energy to make petunia seeds.

Just-past-pink clouds are washing over us above. The wind attends to grace notes.

A tree, trunk at least two inches thick, is growing straight out of the northeastern corner of this brick building—out of the outer wall of my kitchen. Ah, then. I'm put to the test. Who am I rooting for? That tree's rooting for itself, for use. More than cheering, it's grabbing hold and holding on, digging for secrets or nutrients here in these bricks. It's rooting for its own fruit, flowers, leaves. It's rooting for its parasites, and I'm rooting for what feeds off me; I'm rooting for what I want to feed; I'm rooting for my own strength; ever I'm digging my long wooden fingers in.

sunrise 168
5:30 A.M. JUNE 6

clean: clean as a ring

o day, o dawning dance: light and unstrung and unlasting and ring ring ring ring ring ring ring

sunrise 169
5:30 A.M. JUNE 7

There have been a few changes.

O say, can you see something? Say, can you see anything out there?

So start with the faltering window. Start with what you can see through the wavering window. Start with a cold rationale for this semi-poetic monstrosity. Start with what you don't care to admit.

sunrise 170
5:30 A.M. JUNE 8

These are the windows: they rattle and stick. Tall, two-paned and bare, they restrict. They are the lenses; they're strict.

It isn't yet dawn: the sky gleaming mauve midway up the window. Above, one smudge of cloud's darker than the sky that surrounds and suspends it.

Will I get sick here in the winter?

To the west, bricks, chalky and faraway red, catch the west-stretching sunlight and boast it; they boast of it, bright against the still-dusky low-glowing blue.

I sit down to peach yogurt and a fast-paling east.

sunrise 171
5:30 A.M. JUNE 9

Sometimes light seems be made up of
particles. They hurtle through space, into the
earth's atmosphere, then they bounce off
whatever they touch, and the pigments surrender, confessing.

sunrise 172
5:29 A.M. JUNE 10

I slept in a room with a west-facing window.
(Have you heard enough about windows?
They block; they frame; they select, sift, see,
open.)

It's cool out.

There was a time when I despised all but the
wildest of flowers. I didn't calculate this
stance, and I certainly never embraced it.
Cultivated gardens unnerved me. Enough
sense lingered that the rising revulsion at
gardening sections of stores, the alarm at the
flower names (petunia, begonia, tiger lily,
Gerber daisy, hydrangea)—itself repulsed
and alarmed me. I did not ask for this.

I grow flowers now, flowers in pots and in
windows, wherever, and I cannot remember
whether the deadly sense of alarm faded or
fled or whether I willed it away.

The sky above's blue now. I'm going back
in. I want one more hour of sleep.

sunrise 173
5:29 A.M.   JUNE II

lie lie lie lie lie lie lie lie

lie abed lie abed DUMPTRUCK DUMPTRUCK

sunrise 174
5:29 A.M.   JUNE 12

These mornings are loud and unmorninglike.
Clamor
       stretches meaning,
        sifts morning,
       and shifts definition.
The gravity exerted by the object of greater mass
            and the momentum of the traveling object
      strive, do their math, and an orbit results.
Gravity holds definition in place.
      Meanwhile, momentum,
        that gaping bright need to go out out out out out,
   stretches limits to breaking,
        burns at the boundaries,
        builds cities
         (crowding people together
     and keeping them up at night partying),
    and brings in the dumptrucks.

sunrise 175
5:29 A.M.   JUNE 13

Rising sun; mounding lantana.

sunrise 176
5:29 A.M. JUNE 14

Out east the clouds are billowing; this
doesn't make them look soft. Clouds are
only air and wet and something about light.
These are lemon, lucent, high-flung, neither
soft nor dry.

sunrise 177
5:29 A.M. JUNE 15

A circumference is three hundred and sixty
degrees, or two pi radians. (A radian is a
measure equal to a circle's radius.) We work
with degrees, when we take measurements
ruled by the sun. These are inexact, as radians would be, since we haven't any true circles.

sunrise 178
5:29 A.M. JUNE 16

Bread? Earth? I tell you, it is solid. Test it
with your weight. Test it with greater weight.
Take, eat—taste and see.

Just before daybreak, a tightness, and then a
slow-opening.

sunrise 179
5:30 A.M. JUNE 17

They were asking the wrong questions.
They were asking the right questions;
they were asking the wrong way. We
stood in their factory of a back room—
coffee grinders, meat grinders, book
binders, paper slicers—eavesdropping
as we consulted our own records digi-
tally.

sunrise 180
5:30 A.M. JUNE 18

There will be no rush; nothing comes
automatically. There may well be a
rush, but not automatically. Judge by
what you turn to. Keep the bellows
blowing, and water the plants.

sunrise 181

Light obscures.

During the day, we can see farther across into what is near, within our own atmosphere; at night we can see farther out (stars that the sun hides, Jupiter, the Perseids). This is one way in which light obscures. This is not blasphemy; this is observation. Light casts its blanket, its sand over everything it can, and then we see. Light travels; darkness doesn't.

Light is the Magellan, the finder-out, the journalist, the diurnal diarist, the tell-all. Light works with what it has, and it does not wait.

sunrise 182

5:30 A.M.   JUNE 20

Midsummer's Eve: Everyone was sweating. Was the wedding at eleven? We had a little air conditioning, a little shade while we waited. The morning swelled unto midday, swelling with heat, sweltering, swelling with everyone's unfeigned felicity.

sunrise 183

Solstice.

I ate an orange, the lights all still out. Lit the left front eye of the stove to boil water for coffee. I brushed my teeth in the dark and returned to the kitchen at the kettle's shrill summons. The kitchen was dark, the left front eye glowing. The French press is glass. I poured slowly, afraid it would break. I am an apothecary. I held the kettle in my right hand, the tiny press in my left. The press's handle snapped. A little coffee spilled onto the floor. I set the press down, finished filling it, mopped up the spilled coffee. I snapped the handle back over the rim of the glass. I dressed; I pressed and poured the coffee, locked and left the apartment. Went back for the coffee. Locked up again.

It's after five now, but the sky isn't rosy at all. Have I been dreaming all these recent mornings? Have I been looking out the wrong window? Traffic signals flash, some red and some yellow, warning and trusting the few nighttime drivers.

Dead pigeon on the sidewalk. I hear a mourning dove. Another bird, one I can't identify, spills its tangled bright ribbons of song.

As I cross the bridge over the interstate, I don't trust my depth perception. I look down anyhow.

An ambulance waits in the McDonald's drive-thru. Across the street, a man in his neon emergency gear has gone jogging.

At 5:40, I sit down at the steps of the Customs House. At 5:37, as I came over the hill at 9th Avenue, I finally saw the sun, easing its distance, inch over the purple far treelined horizon.

Generally, I speak to the strangers I pass.

sunrise 184
5:30 A.M. JUNE 22

Where is this heating-and-air-unit window
getting its stories, anyway?

I don't live miles above the street, but I'm
higher up than the ground floor. Yesterday I
was down on the street; I couldn't see light
like this (orange and bright) until I'd walked
several blocks. But from here—

My brother once returned a quarter to the
local bank when he saw they'd over-credited
his account by as much. Where can I return
my quarter?

sunrise 185
5:31 A.M. JUNE 23

You sobered me up with the kind of sobriety
often mistaken for drunkenness. You bore
through my thoughts and my words as a
deft-handled drill drills bits down into wood-
en beams, fastening. You fractured my right
leg: only a coward would hide because my
limp is ghastly. It's ghastly, indeed. Am I
skilled, now, at haunting? I am wealthy and
upright enough to be stolen from.

A word about the weather: It is chilly; it is
cloudy. I am wrapped up in a blanket. This
summer could shiver the truth out of anyone.

sunrise 186
5:31 A.M.   JUNE 24

Jacob wrestled with the Angel of the Lord until dawn.

Until dawn, I slept; at dawn I wrestled. My foe wasn't angelic: not beatific, that is—a mighty messenger, certainly. No one changed my name or my life. From self to self with perfect precision the alarm relayed the message: "Wake up—five o'clock." The precision lay in the relay alone. The code was faulty, or I'm faulty—fumbling, resisting. All the while the world's dawning. I prevailed, though what I gained from the win wasn't much.

sunrise 187
5:31 A.M.   JUNE 25

Surely other kids were rattled, too, though I don't recall any eruptions of panic, only a slight swell of collective agitation. We found out that while our sun was young yet, it wasn't so very young, and the diagram made plain where things were headed. Over billions of years—so the science book said—the sun would get hotter and fatter; by the time it'd become a Red Giant, it would've swallowed us whole.

Main sequence stars—that's ours—"have achieved a hydrostatic equilibrium, where the forces of gravity trying to collapse the star are balanced by the energy released from the fusion reactions trying to blow the star apart." Who writes these books? Was someone trying to blow us apart? We were young, but no longer so very young.

sunrise 188
5:32 A.M. JUNE 26

The sun rose uncontested. Who'd contest it?
Anyone tired or reluctant to barrel down
into (through) death, that "final smashup"
Jean Mermoz assures us is "worth it." Curtains would contest the sun; so would doors
and blinds that shut and clouds that smother,
diffusing. All the while the uncontested sun
itself "shines" imperviously, existing (uncontested) at some violent "equilibrium," itself
contested ever from within, without—

A sphere is the most compact shape possible.

sunrise 189
5:32 A.M. JUNE 27

Having come down from the solstice I've a
slight sense, manufactured perhaps, heady
nonetheless, of going downhill. Having
come down from my tower I can see out further east: horizons draped with a haze, far
clouds lit in thin neon streaks.

Out from behind the building at the end of
this street, the sun, like—forgive me—a
cookie, a stoplight, a resplendent red balloon, eases, eases on out. Slow and conspic-
uous, fat and gelatinous, it's easing out into
the center of the street.

sunrise 190

Every day rests neatly
on its yesterday,
atop
a high
gyrating
stack
of yesterdays.
The tower's gyrating,
but it's not about to fall;
the pieces are
magnetic,
and the base,
low away though it be,
holds solid.

Sometimes there are eclipses, and we marvel.
We wonder what they'll do to our crops,
our retinas,
our fates.

Each day eclipses
the one before;
every year eclipses
the last. One scene or two from other years—from memory—
may threaten to eclipse
all future possibilities, all workable, happily
alternate constructs.

But if the days are magnetic stacked blocks,
it could be that thing you can't forget
works invisibly
to structure the tower,
in all its fine gyration.
With every endeavor,
you return to a theme.
Another day dawns,
and every sunrise is that one,

or else every sunrise
is *to* that one
so conspicuously   parallel.
You start to curse   this automatic
organization   of thought—
did you pay to have this particular,
particular   filter   installed?
The pattern may make for a handy motif;
it doesn't make the air any cleaner.

Look out the window: look *out*. Stare into the sun
if you will, if you can. It may burn
something away. It may change the shape
of your language, your grammar,
your too-personal blessing or curse of a filter.
(You don't know what it may burn away.
You don't know what it may harden and set.)

sunrise 191
5:33 A.M. JUNE 29

Suddenly light flooded the kitchen.

I cracked a boiled egg at the window.

sunrise 192
5:33 A.M. JUNE 30

If your eye is single, your whole body will
be full of light.

sunrise 193
5:34 A.M.   JULY 1

I open the door, and "ooo—ooo—," says the
far traffic, at a concert B. The morning is
cool and unjunelike, cool and unjulylike.
The tortoise-shell cat stares from her perch,
anxious, deciding. The traffic tones widen:
"ooh-ee, ooh-ee," "mmmm …" still moan-
ing and musical.

sunrise 194
5:34 A.M.   JULY 2

Thunder with the sunrise: cows, howling. I
wring my hands as if I'm washing them, to
warm and to liven them up again. 5:59 rain
(on the back of my wrist). The sky is closing,
closing, closing. And rain—on the back of
my right hand, an inch below my index
knuckle.

sunrise 195
5:35 A.M.   JULY 3

The distant burning pink
    affects the nearer green.
The green leaves, right
    there out my window?
In this still-early light
    they're bluer than usual.
Far rose-fire light
    lights them translucent
        and red.

sunrise 196
5:35 A.M.   JULY 4

A minute before five, yellow city light dusts the window. Beyond that, the scraggly tree; beyond that, a dual-toned sky: blue above, rose below.

Should I go out?

I put on the old dress, the one with the lace.

Morning spreads into the house. Do I need to go out? It's 5:17 now; the eastern sky has ripened to a dusty pink. I'm boiling water for coffee; in the oven bread's toasting.

Stepped out the back door. I fear the petunias aren't going to make it. The kettle whistles. The water boils fast. This stove heats pretty quickly. Before I can pour coffee into the press, I hear my alarm. Time to catch the sunrise.

There's a breeze. The Picasso scarf stirs in the window.

sunrise 197
5:36 A.M.   JULY 5

Recalled, by the morning orange light, this trinket: the way one thing will reachingly (long and soft tendrils) take care of everything; and this one: that everything faithfully pertains to one thing (weblike, hublike). Recalled, by such orange light, the reaching leap required to affirm or deny, considering the wide way everything stretches out, out so far, beyond all discernible limit.

sunrise 198
5:36 A.M. JULY 6

Enheartened by a complex song, I stand expanding, senses widening into this allotted vastness: mountain view, hilly field, thumbnail moon high in the eastern sky.

I shiver—sweet, cool, defiant July—and shudder. The shudder doesn't belong here.

Examining a patch of houndstooth on this quilt—When will the pattern sit well with me? This isn't a case of plain checkered squares; the light and dark here claw into each other, neither one seeming to mind very much.

Here's the sun, orange, east, north.

sunrise 199
5:37 A.M. JULY 7

"Revoke!"—this whispered, with scarcely an object in mind.

(westfacing westfacing westfacing westfacing—turn turn turn turn)

The western sky panel, too, dawns. I could go downstairs for coffee, but I hear someone. A minute past six, I eye a slim reflection on brass or fake brass lampstand.

These mornings are portals.

sunrise 200
5:37 A.M. JULY 8

The ghost cries out for gold, when all I've got here is straw—and so I spin, spin the sorry light. The ghost leans at the door with an outward look of imploring and in an even tone demands alchemy. I tell him that alchemists discovered the active ingredient in aspirin. They couldn't turn copper and iron into gold or mix any elixir of life; they never could reach their great hope, but they happened upon an easy way to dull their pain.

Day breaks at the periphery.

sunrise 201
5:38 A.M. JULY 9

So this is how morning breaks anyway, after whatever the night. I meet it open-handedly; I meet it openly, despite my instinctive constriction at the recognition.

No day's a good day to be powerless. The petunias have dried up. I don't want any coffee.

"Weeping may endure for a night; joy comes in the morning." So it goes. Nights may endure for months, years, but even so. If you give it enough sturdy chances—hold open all the right windows—joy will come around eventually; it'll come home and let itself in.

sunrise 202
5:38 A.M. JULY 10

Dawn: awe with an awl, awl with a caul—
call no one (not now, not at this hour)—our
hourly awe awaits (there in the jerked-open
junk drawer). Draw the drapes.

Draw water. Draw straws—the one with the
shortest straw loses forever. Go on; get along
now (long for no one). Long day? Long for
no day.

sunrise 203
5:39 A.M. JULY 11

Dawn is an awl: It is sharp. It pierces
the night; hue lockstitches it
leather-like right
to the day.

sunrise 204
5:40 A.M. JULY 12

Dawn (awl and all) is kind, cobalt, quiet, stark.

sunrise 205
5:40 A.M. JULY 13

Dawn stole in. Dawn climbed feet-first in through the window and stood soaking and blue in the corner, dripping, self-satisfied, in from the thunder.

sunrise 206
5:41 A.M. JULY 14

Defeat's not a thing to rise out of; it's a thing to rise through. It gathers as a mist, may block vision, cannot restrict motion.

The day begins with a demand. The demand's wrapped inside an invitation, a sharp knife wrapped in a calico dishtowel.

The sun's not the Messiah, though its rising can be like his coming. Who or what am I rising to meet? Exactly. I rise for a sight, and I rise for a reckoning. Enough.

sunrise 207
5:42 A.M. JULY 15

If this is a game, then I want to keep playing.

sunrise 208

The enzyme Pol V is characterized by an "economy of motion and a quickness to engage." Translesion synthesis: save what you can, while you can, while there's still time. Don't think too meticulously; just get down your impressions. Nothing's too sacred to save or destroy; let matter take care of itself—but save what you can while the music is churning, before your home-mountain becomes a volcano and takes out the house of your childhood imaginings. Everyone's got to reuse what they've got—a sock once a bracelet, a clamp once a toaster, that commonplace book now a blanket, that shoe once a lemonade stirring-spoon—and so on. So copy it quickly—yes, you'll get mutations; you'll probably like them eventually. Learn to view scars as cosmetic entities, windfall tattoos, or calligraphic autographs of people or events that you admire. Learning to live with inclusion is difficult: you must include everyone who has betrayed you, or you will forever feel vengeful, and then you will shrivel, I'm telling you. "Some of the accidental mutations are likely to be helpful."

sunrise 209

The cattle cry out in antiphony.

sunrise 210
5:44 A.M. JULY 18

The mist lends a hoariness, a quaint air of
wisdom, to the distant rising sun. If from
now on I always prefer sunrises to conversation, will I keep safe? Long, curled
strands of cow-hair hang there, caught on
the barbs in the wire of the fence.

sunrise 211
5:44 A.M. JULY 19

At five, it's still a night sky, blackberry. I
set water to boil, step out the back door.
Faint-illumed clouds brush past high overhead. They're lit dim rose-yellow; wind's
blowing them east. A small but steady
breeze: I'm chilled. I welcome the chill.
(Shiver off the nagging memories that surface in the skin—)

The city is conspiring with July.

I turn off the stove's eye and put on my
shoes. I can still meet the sunrise at 9th if I
go ahead and leave now. The city below
swells gently into a cold sweat. Some fever
is breaking. The clouds all hang violet and
cool.

sunrise 212
5:45 A.M. JULY 20

Yesterday I walked downtown to catch
the action, but the violet sky was secretive. Jaded, I stayed in this morning. By
the look of the patch of sky visible from
the fire escape, that secretive violet
burst into orange violence, twisting
streaks of a visual battle-cry over 9th
Avenue.

(So the electric alarm interrupts the
most convincing dream, and any buried
secret may burst into full aerial view.)

sunrise 213
5:46 A.M. JULY 21

Cling to data so to climb.
Often there are footholds.
Lines connecting eyes (or
any organ of perception) to trees,
the windowsill, the western sky, the eastern sky,
the road below—they act as ropes. This is a net;
they hold us somewhat steady. Every datum (sweet, discrete)
is duly reported. I have an uncountable number of secretaries.

sunrise 214
5:46 A.M. JULY 22

The air's a cloud of dust,
a mass of matter that's transparent,
a mass of delivery men. The men lug the light, hoisting it,
hefting it off their backs, off their shoulders, rolling it
heavy and hard from one back to another.
The particles are faithful to transmit,
faulty in their transcription,
steadfast to translate,
strict to refract.

sunrise 215
5:47 A.M. JULY 23

The break of morning was all sound: the moan of the traffic,
the moan of the train, the roar of the good-morning dumptruck. Dawn broke unsound, unsteady and soft.

sunrise 216
5:48 A.M. JULY 24

The ants are too close to my back door again. The coffee's a
version of perfect. The yellow lantana's indomitable. This
day's a table, spread with the day's things: a cup of coffee,
lantana, ants, a test, a schedule, some friends, dead ants, a
remnant of a dream, some books, the mail, a floor I need to
sweep.

I wake, and the sky is still dark, blue-dark. I wake, and the
dawn's turning it plum. I wake: out the window, rose-
soaked nectarine. I wake again: day's begun; the sky's blue,
lit. I stay with a dream another moment. It's 6:15. I get up
to make coffee. I sit down to the table.

sunrise 217
5:49 A.M.   JULY 25

A large black bee is wearing itself out at the
window, beating and beating against the
glass. The window is open; the bee flew in a
minute ago. Did it come for the Picasso
scarf, expecting a flower so large?

He dropped—out of exhaustion?—down to
the opening, caught the breeze, and dipped
silently out.

And the still-young day's a stubborn dog,
shedding, sweating, panting, lolling on the
carpet, nuzzling at your foot insistently.

sunrise 218
5:49 A.M.   JULY 26

At five, rise.
Run your right
or left hand
across
the mantelpiece.
Fumble
at the mantelpiece.
Reach
into your pocket.
Dig deep
in the quiet tight
blue and dark pocket,
and pull out
the sun.

sunrise 219
5:50 A.M. JULY 27

Day broke unspoken. City towers taper upward, spikes speaking what might otherwise stay secret.

Since this time last year, the sun's spun us
all 'round, the hub of a wheel with invisible
spokes.

Pormpuraawans, who live on Australia's
Cape York Peninsula, when asked to order
pictures chronologically, consistently arrange them from east to west.

I have to see. I flip the switch, though the
kitchen light's garish against all this blue.

sunrise 220
5:51 A.M. JULY 28

Night reveals stars; day hides them. Come,
sun, invade us.

We're all headed east. We were driven,
eastward, from the garden. No turning
back, we're still headed east. East, east,
east, east, on to something else, on to
something further if not greater, on to
something brighter, maybe—east into
whatever brightness we can find, whatever
brightness we can stand, with only an overcast notion that in moving forward and
onward, we might break through night ourselves someday (rising), come full circle
home.

sunrise 221

Back back back back back up into sense.
If sense consists
    of networked definitions,
        of competency, back up further,
be thought senseless.

You'll have to return, but
you'll have prefaced and purified
speech with immediacy.

Wrestle the dawn into day.

sunrise 222

When I woke, the morning was blue yet, and
dark. The insistent and painfully faithful
alarm heralded the new day from the hard-
to-find place where I left it last night.

I am here, Lord.

Drowse and dark wrapped me tight, pulled
me back under. The sun rose before I did.
The dumptruck (also so faithful) didn't fail
to inform me.

Well. Well, here it is. The day is bright, the
breeze is soft, and facts lie where they've
fallen. The having-happeneds all take root,
or else they fossilize.

sunrise 223
5:53 A.M. JULY 31

The sky's awash with drifting, granulating
clouds. Earlier, a storm rolled through: the
morning's well-washed. Now, the clouds at
the low western horizon are lit wisteria.

I'm out on the porch, eating cherries.

If I can memorize everything there is to see
about these birds, maybe Dad can tell me
their species.

A gibbous moon hangs overhead, overhead
and west. Its waning isn't even. The curve's
not smooth; it's pinched, and nearly pointed.

sunrise 224
5:54 A.M. AUGUST 1

The barest description built of the wrong words
will come for you in the night. Behind the clouds,
the sun's simple rim shines
as dull and as thin and precise as a wafer.
The petunias are scraggly
in their mismatched pots, placed to weigh down
rag rugs on the fire escape landing.
Yesterday's rain weighs them down deeper.
That bright wafer
will not be weighed down,
not by mismatched words or faulty insistence.
The faulty insistence will break under
weight.

sunrise 225
5:55 A.M. AUGUST 2

The rugs on the fire escape have dried out. Under a plain early sky stand the lantana and cleome, green, bare of petals.

sunrise 226
5:56 A.M. AUGUST 3

Dawn is more faithful than honest. I am more honest than faithful. Language is more hard-pressed than architectural.

The architect told us that he liked small things, "like the sky." The roof opened up, the walls fell away (mechanically, not by magic), and we stood on a dark shore in the night breeze, waves breaking. Using primitive equipment, the man began to demonstrate how we might take three-inch photos of the cloud-shrouded pink moon.

sunrise 227
5:56 A.M. AUGUST 4

The astrophysicist C. Alex Young said that when it's hit with enough force, the earth's magnetosphere rings like a bell.

In the sun, magnetic field lines twist and tangle. Sometimes they snap, and a piece of the sun hurtles outward, hits our atmospheric gong—We're ringing, wondering. In 1859, the telegraph system failed. Some people never got their messages. In 1989, the entire Quebec power grid went out. Compasses can fail, too.

I bobbed to the top of the night sea, set the daybell ringing, shut off the alarm with unalert affection.

sunrise 228
5:57 A.M. AUGUST 5

The line of the mist is smooth and self-certain.

sunrise 229
5:58 A.M. AUGUST 6

I woke to beating rain. It fell in sheets, in waves, and the rotating fan sent waves my way. At five, the room held more light than full night; by six, morning had come in, spread out, filled the house.

sunrise 230
5:59 A.M. AUGUST 7

Everything's spinning
  to conserve
old momentum.

I wake every morning to
  opportunities ripe for betrayal,
perched
on the window ledge like late-summer peaches,
  flesh tender and tempting,
and oh,
  the rough fuzz in the mouth,
the rip,
the tear,
  the summer-sweet juice spilling out.
I could trade gardening Eden for being like God,
  trade birthright for supper,
trade sweat of life-mission for
  wilderness breakfast.

sunrise 231
6:00 A.M. AUGUST 8

Waking dew-wet / limping, accented /
innocent menacing / gift-wrapped
proportion / one false and first
and reassuring ray.

sunrise 232

It was early as ever, and I was tired, so I brewed coffee to construct my own welcome. I laid out a wide welcome-mat, filled the kitchen with pineapples.

Against slate sapphire overhead, clouds dully glowed a heavy yellow, close to color of smog. Gradually, further-up pieces appeared, a white pink. The sky showed its dimensions, progressively and over time, the way folk will.

As soon as I could see well enough without it—around six—I turned off the kitchen light.

From just out the door, I spied a lime glow to the east. I ran to another place for a better look. It was artificial light, flung against the wide outer wall of a parking garage.

Back in the kitchen, I ate all the pineapples except four: one to save, three to throw to the squirrels.

sunrise 233
6:01 A.M. AUGUST 10

If you cannot do without symmetry, set light in the darkness against sound in the silence.

Sound through the darkness is not quite as welcome as coffee. Light through the silence is welcome with nary a question unless you are after a deep and dense sleep.

sunrise 234
6:02 A.M.   AUGUST II

If you want to, take your eyes out, and wrap them up in all that pink.

Four or five kittens, tiny enough that such ferocious insistence surprises, all fuzz and eyes and claws, fought as a fuzz-and-claw storm to get out the cracked-open back door.

sunrise 235
6:03 A.M.   AUGUST I2

These are bundles of rays, cities of rays, forcing their way west. West! As if the impervious sun cared for our wests. The violet has flown, and this is a persed yellow dawn.

sunrise 236
6:04 A.M.   AUGUST 13

There are no feats of will here.
Nothing to see here.
These are feats
of nothing, or else
feats of grace.

The morning consists
of dawn, chill, sunrise, coffee,
and toward neighboring dawns, a sisterly
insistence on constancy.
Substance lies
in what sinks, not what rises.
The coffee grounds are pressed
to the base of the cylinder.
The morning's subsistence, after the light, consists
of a boiled egg and strong coffee.

sunrise 237
6:04 A.M.   AUGUST 14

We weren't sure of the way, but we were
sure we could find it.

sunrise 238
6:05 A.M.   AUGUST 15

from thick sleep up into a wall
   or pile of bricks, and from the bricks
a vine or a tree, and from the sky a light,
   and from the plastic planter, a vine
that some night
   might
bloom

sunrise 239
6:06 A.M. AUGUST 16

I am sitting in the kitchen, not walking down the street. I am sitting in the kitchen with coffee. A friend recommended some parks from which I might watch the sunrise: Maybe on a weekend morning, a little closer to fall. Maybe after the equinox.

Outside it's overcast, cool, and lovely. Outside are vines that twist upon themselves as tangles, flames, or frantic thoughts.

sunrise 240
6:07 A.M. AUGUST 17

The morning's tough and fibrous, pithy, sweet-stinging and bright as a pineapple core.

I tried pineapple core during the time when I kept trying the parts of fruits and vegetables people typically discard. I ate an apple core first, and it seemed like a good idea—that started it—then it was pear cores, the stems of spinach leaves, bell pepper seeds, the dried skin of red onions, tomato leaves. The throwing-out of stems, skins, seeds, or leaves I regarded a sort of injustice.

sunrise 241
6:08 A.M. AUGUST 18

Occasionally a dream, constructing vivid, believable scenes from those of stories, from wishes and memories, always on old and potent themes, will promise a new and seemingly workable resolution. But the dream is an ethereal, electrical thing, and it cannot deliver. The long-awaited and longed-for meeting-again happens. What happens after that? Your scrambling brain, caught up in the distractions of longing, of resolving to forget and of forgetting, in the mechanics of REM, forgot to plan. There is nowhere stored data detailing a convincing and workable conclusion. The dream ends in an irresolution parallel to what actually happened, last year or yesterday, or a decade or half-decade or half-century back.

I wake to a bodily sense of believing or wanting to believe a promise, or the sense of looking up from the picture book, when I was young, and wondering when I might wear long dresses and fly and whether there were goblins in the closet—I wake gently, to granulated light, minutes old by the time we meet.

sunrise 242
6:08 A.M. AUGUST 19

We'll welcome the light, that scattered ambassador
        of a distant sun—We'll invite him to come in for tea.
The rain was here first, but we've a whole steaming kettle here,
        and an extra chair—

sunrise 243
6:09 A.M. AUGUST 20

Moan, train, moan, go on—We've got plenty to
hear when we hear you.

The sun shone too far north. I knew something
was off. The sunrise was a reflection off wide
and high southerly windows.

sunrise 244
6:10 A.M. AUGUST 21

Mums can speak of color, because they have a
luminous brightness, as if they are so eager for
light, so photosynthetically hungry, that they
rob their surroundings of what would otherwise
be an even distribution of photons. The yellow
ones are the worst. Oh, but I do not write to ac-
cuse them! *Au contraire*, they have my love, my
regard! They more than survive.

sunrise 245
6:11 A.M. AUGUST 22

There were seven years of plenty; yesterday was
one: the world inside a hazelnut, a year in a
morning or in a red onion. One could die of surfeit. I haven't died of dearth or surfeit yet.

Dawn's cold: cool, soon to be colder. I opened
the back door to cool off the kitchen; I opened
the oven to warm it back up.

sunrise 246

Just over the dark, dirty green of the brick,
dawn shone pink. My eye met this sky as if
it were a living thing—a twisting vine, or a
small cat.

sunrise 247

This city does sleep—
fitfully. This city dozes.
Streetlights flash yellow
or red for eight hours; colorful
gathering places close up for the night,
and traffic dies down. The sun rises,
then people do. The ones up at dawn or before
have spent nervous nights in apartments, on balconies
and porches, on sidewalks and benches, in the one café
that doesn't close, or they're getting up to run,
or they're getting up to drive.
Invisibly, Orion's rising.
One vine winds
    through the window
and into the kitchen.

sunrise 248
6:13 A.M. AUGUST 25

I ran my hand
  along the mantelpiece,
toward the window.
I could tell
  that the dawn
and dark
  hold secrets.
They are small
  bundles:
spherical
  bags filled taut
with something warm
  and soft.
They'll pack
  by hundreds into
    tight corners;
they'll crowd
    by tens into
  your palm.

sunrise 249
6:14 A.M. AUGUST 26

Out the high western window, a moon and a
star. By electric light I taste the soup. Outside, three more purple buds have appeared
on the moon vine. The soup isn't done yet; I
pour a bowl anyway. I turn out the light.
The moon sets; the star hides.

sunrise 250
6:15 A.M. AUGUST 27

Be inspired—be
  breathed into.
To choose that which uplifts
and challenges will drain and exhaust;
  it will not destroy. This is choosing flight
                              and fire.
                    Spread self as tent,
                        parachute,
                      membrane, balloon;
          be filled with hot air; be lifted and driven;
                                be moved.
The hole or void is starving for an antecedent, for a reason.
    If we can't pin down the pronoun,
if we can't make it confess
    or say, well—we'll ride the upward
                          current
                of the adjective.

sunrise 251
6:16 A.M. AUGUST 28

Just past this pane
  wind tiny dried
    curls of vines.
  Most of the vines
      on this brick heap
        are foliate;
      these
  aren't alive.
  The vines
      were afraid,
    or someone
          was
        afraid
          of the vines.

sunrise 252
6:16 A.M. AUGUST 29

up up up / plummet

sunrise 253
6:17 A.M. AUGUST 30

Freeze the day for later. Summon it up when you like. The sun'll rise, invited or not, to your private high summit, unless you're tight-sealed in a thick-walled box or hidden somewhere underground.

sunrise 254
6:18 A.M. AUGUST 31

Songs given at night will bury themselves (as seeds do) in the dark in you, to shoot a shoot up come morning. Come, give them water.

sunrise 255

Last night, the moon vine bloomed.
For a couple days now, the green,
>> twisted bud
>> has protruded
>> from its tiny purple
>> calyx;
>> last night
>> it opened, wide,
>> pale and fragrant, while
> we were away
> in the parlor.
Talk about songs in the night.

By the time I
> met it this morning, the fragile
>> pink petals had begun
>> to shrivel.
The ferns on the roof
> are still hardy.
The mornings pack their punches.
Pack a bag of punches;
> pack a bag of plums.
Talk about songs in the night.

sunrise 256

Mums bloom against the chill—It is their
boast and their exercise.

sunrise 257
6:20 A.M. SEPTEMBER 3

I am so young, and those are uneven cows.
There is no secret lilt that I know of. Every
lilt is a limp transferred to the mouth and
resulting in hobbling. Hobble, then, fine.
Finer to hobble than strut (for the telling of
secrets). This is the sky: it is low-slung, a
wide and unraveled soft ribbon, and all of
one color. And this is the air: it is early September. And this is the wood: it is gray and
separated while honest and green and insistent. And this is the hill: it is low; it is green;
there are cows. And this is the mountain: the
color is just off the blue hour. And this is the
yard: there are Birds, and the Maple sheds
early its leaves, without turning, because it is
tired, and it is relieved. And this is the cup: it
is given. And this is the cow: it is risen. And
this is the pear tree: it welcomes the birds.
And this is the cat: it is black. And this is the
day: it dawns, ceaselessly. And this is the
chair: Adirondack. And this is the young
day: perched on the doorstep. And this is
love: deliberate, then irrevocable. And this is
the sky: it is a pearl, and concave.

sunrise 258
6:21 A.M. SEPTEMBER 4

Am I unabashedly strategic? No. I am abashedly so.

sunrise 259
6:22 A.M. SEPTEMBER 5

I'll take one hammer, one chisel—oh—three
chisels, please. I'll be hammering hard. I can
pay you in calluses. I've no marble here, but
this pile of concrete will yield at first light.

sunrise 260
6:23 A.M. SEPTEMBER 6

A small circle of light hit the curve of the oil-
pastel malachite mountain, right where the
sun would've risen.

Mindful of cyclical time, I wrapped up in a
shawl to shield myself from the chill of
mornings past and mornings to come as
much as the near-autumn air.

sunrise 261
6:23 A.M. SEPTEMBER 7

Vision's a pane of thinnest glass, both sides
burning.

sunrise 262
6:24 A.M. SEPTEMBER 8

A squirrel's silhouette guards the window.

I lay back down diagonally.

The moon vine's second flower has wilted significantly. I break its stalk, place it in water, hide it in the shadows under the bed. Lost love is a useless motif. The drops from the faucet are fat. I'll water everything by grief.

I take the coffee to the parlor. Clementine light pours in from the street, muted blue from the sky. No one else lives here—There is no one to tighten my breath against. I tighten my breath against myself, against notions and images. Be ever-unloading, ever-awaiting, ever-adjusting, ever-constructing.

sunrise 263
6:25 A.M. SEPTEMBER 9

Late? We've only crumbs left; some have fallen. Do you care for crumbs that fall? Come, take a plate; take a napkin. Care for a simulacrum? Come, sit. You can view a thing or two from inside this clouded solitude, or you can watch the screen, or you can dream. The hardest warmth crumbled into a shiver.

sunrise 264
6:26 A.M. SEPTEMBER 10

The nerve lies on ice, stretches out in the cold.
The nerve doesn't lie but
hears the squirrels
       and reports.
Chill dispels
vague notions in favor of bodily jolt.

Give me some grounds for wild hope.
Wanted: grounds for wild hope.
Wanted: wild hope.

sunrise 265
6:26 A.M. SEPTEMBER 11

Sound can't cross void like light, so all solar storms and everyday plasmic roars re-
main secret, stranded, untranslated. All
round the water-wet rock, days meet the fat
mute fiery visitor with an array of oblivious
this-worldly promenades. This morning's is
quiet: crickets, a few birds, muted traffic.

Near seven, the near-equinoctial sun has
risen to idly finger a cloth of blue cloud,
then wrap up in it, leaving a smear of
pearlescent pink just below. This space of
pearl gives way to righteous white cumulus, opening out into early-day open-sky
over the mountain.

sunrise 266
6:27 A.M. SEPTEMBER 12

sound
light
air   star
sun   color   heat
cloud   dawn
dark
daybreak

Give the kaleidoscope a good shake.
Infinity's a tease; these mornings are both short and numbered.

sunrise 267
6:28 A.M. SEPTEMBER 13

Stepped into the kitchen. One light in the
hotel went out.

sunrise 268
6:29 A.M. SEPTEMBER 14

When we level the playing field, will we level the pitcher's mound, too?

Earth is un-tilting as its year unwinds. Give
us a week and some days, and we'll hold the
Sun up at the zenith. If the Sun cared a thing
for the earth, the Sun might well exult. Some
toe-shoe-clad foot will balance on a red
autumnal point, and we'll all have the same
night.

sunrise 269
6:30 A.M. SEPTEMBER 15

This room is blue until around seven, when the sun, risen, lights the purple katanga strung across the window, and the whole room glows yellow and amethyst.

Every night I have to hide my face from the streetlights below. I need heavier drapes.

From this hole of an island,
   from this ivory tower or rickety rented room,
      from this cavernous box of white paint,
                           sink,

                              sing,

                                 see.

sunrise 270
6:30 A.M. SEPTEMBER 16

The sun's staking out the south section of sky.
We're living off-peak, living low,
                  laying low,
                     living in low demand.
The summer solstice has long gone.
         The ground isn't solid; it's volatile, untrustworthy.
                Peaks can erupt from below, fold and fault you.

(You know that he will come,
and he will trip over your things; he will admire
and then brush up against the monuments you've propped
      too precariously against open doors and rocking-chair legs,
               so that the monuments topple.)

sunrise 271
6:31 A.M. SEPTEMBER 17

A place for everything
   and everything in its place;
a name for everything
   and everything by its name,
     answering to its name,
or moved dumb and unwilling about by its name.

Rootless and restless
  as anyone, I own only what I
        see: I own all I see.

Chimes order the morning,
  owning the hour, announcing the breeze.
Language is proprietary, but the soul of things is free.

Before night left, he kicked yellow crumbs
                 across the eastern sky.

sunrise 272
6:32 A.M. SEPTEMBER 18

All summer long the plants have withered
and rallied, withered and rallied again.

sunrise 273
6:33 A.M. SEPTEMBER 19

Dawn's unassailable, hard and bright.

The sails lie together, heavy and crumpled; we're
not going anywhere soon.

sunrise 274

Woke before the flower closed, an amber haze
about us both.

The how, the how, the how to, the what to—

One possible answer's a dream: in which
someone unlikely offers an ongoing kindness,
or in which a small spot of radiance spreads to
cover a whole sphere of dark blue, or in which
hoops of metal dissolve without warning.

sunrise 275

The tree out back is drawing in its water, a
yearly tide that leaves behind (in leaves) the
xanthophyll that's been there, dim and secret
behind summer verdure.

sunrise 276
6:35 A.M. SEPTEMBER 22

Give me great distances, chasms to speak across, great to surround me (a wide, wakeful fortress), bounded by far edge of echoing stone.

Last night's flower closes like a fist; I close my fist about the city. Reaching for the sun, I close my hand again against the brightness and heat, a fistful of fire.

The Farmer's Almanac says that the autumnal equinox is today. Dawn rises in fist-swinging revolt; I swing my own fiery fists right back. The year's going down fighting.

It is with trepidation that I step over the edge, following the earth—all right, this here hemisphere—on its descent into darkness and death. I welcomed the fall before it began, back in August, when the apartment started to cool off. But it's with a rising round tension I've watched the leaves fade. The wild vine—the one that wound into the kitchen—is growing less rapidly. The leaves above me rattle, dying while they're yet green. Before they die, they'll tell their secrets, tell all their secret pigments.

We balance, revel, slip, sleep; day falls into the night.

sunrise 277
6:36 A.M. SEPTEMBER 23

Below, the traffic is growling.

Did I build those hotels myself, as a barricade, a shield from direct honest light? I required an apartment with east-facing windows, but this is the city: I didn't fight for a view clear to horizon.

Demeter curses the earth in her sorrow.

sunrise 278
6:37 A.M. SEPTEMBER 24

This season's a bridge
        downward
            and out
                into a sparer space.
                     Sweet
                   exiguity:
           winter's our spare world;
           we can run on reserves.
           (Won't you reserve
           me a table, a time?)

But I am running ahead, across months and bridges. The year's only just begun to turn.

At the edges, things flicker. At the edges of vision and of understanding, and at the edges of tense, nearly congealed air that is the relationship between things or beings—there images are generated, or there things themselves shift and switch, unsteady in their existence.

When looked upon directly, they freeze (for we are all Gorgons). The resulting stones can be painted, cut, connected by strings.

sunrise 279
6:37 A.M. SEPTEMBER 25

The night splinters.
We've come out on top again. Light clatters
                                    to
                                        the
    floor, then lies there,   blurred at the edges and   spreading.

sunrise 280
6:38 A.M. SEPTEMBER 26

Day fell from the ceiling,
            fell from the sky,
crawled across the concrete, scraped its knees, climbed upstairs,
                    lay still on the floor.
        I listened to its breathing before either of us spoke.

sunrise 281
6:39 A.M. SEPTEMBER 27

        Clouds cup us cool and tight. The hour's
        opportune for crime, for subdued or undue
        alarm, for crumbling paint.

sunrise 282
6:40 A.M. SEPTEMBER 28

The hemisphere dragged shadowed and soft against her skin as she spun the blue bead, the largest one on the ribbon-tied bracelet. Her index finger spun the bead with quick-swinging rhythmic jerks as she thought of rosaries, heresies, jump-rope rhymes. The thinning ribbon didn't snap; its strands let go quietly, and four beads rolled away, their clatter muffled by the carpet, before she caught the largest one and enclosed it in her palm.

sunrise 283
6:41 A.M. SEPTEMBER 29

Have I mentioned the cable, thrown up to the roof? Not the roof of the building or atmosphere—higher. There's a fat grappling hook on the end; any day now I'll pull myself up. (The cable's taut. For now, it's enough to jerk it, to feel that it's secure, and to know where it leads.)

No: the line's cast from above, and a hook's hooked in me. So I'm pierced through, but going somewhere.

sunrise 284
6:41 A.M.   SEPTEMBER 30

I wanted to know what it felt like to touch life, to grasp it as dirt, so I ventured one finger, then both my hands. My own blood's on my hands now if I draw back. The world's placid, impassive, and plain. I know that to speak is to change the arrangement, however slight or right the change.

To speak now is to presume to categorize or to add value. I cannot presume. I can't not presume.

Stern world! Fine. I could kick kick kick kick kick make a dent. I could sneeze hard and stir up the sunset tonight. Or, armed with a drill, I could bore into some tender or weak spot (in the wall, in the sky, at the borders of sight, in the language—that net of definitions closing in). I could suck in my stomach, tuck in my feet, close my eyes and become a gaping black pupil myself, and let world and world and world pour through.

sunrise 285
6:42 A.M.   OCTOBER 1

Push the hair out of your face, and seal the stars away.

sunrise 286
6:43 A.M.   OCTOBER 2

What the light's got, at the sill: the good stubborn angle of a crowbar.

sunrise 287
6:44 A.M. OCTOBER 3

The squat, hairy thing had a wide face, sullen eyes, and burnt teeth. I saw it, but I wouldn't speak its name. Know the truth, and the truth will set you free. There are stages of knowing—take care, as you can, what you see; once you've seen what you've seen, take care what and whether you call it.

I knew the thing couldn't follow (This was no great escape.), so I left it and went out down the hall.

sunrise 288
6:45 A.M. OCTOBER 4

Summer's now a chalky mass, cool and dry and crumbling. As the year breaks down, some bird's sending forth small rolling mountains of song.

sunrise 289
6:45 A.M. OCTOBER 5

Passage of time: a railroad crossing and a corridor.

Here is a blade. (If it breaks? There are more in your mouth.) Start digging. Bore through time itself; emerge as a panting refugee diver or a fat ribbon woven through fabric, at spaces called moments. When a moment widens, it's momentous. Choose ye this day which way ye shall dig, for the way that thou diggest shall be the way that thou goest.

sunrise 290
6:46 A.M. OCTOBER 6

listening / bare

Outside on the concrete, I walk atop atop atop and through.

Perception's slow (That is, it is enough of an action that we've taken the trouble of verb.), so I am surprised (That is, I register changes and even feel some small switch flick on, off, in response.).

sunrise 291
6:47 A.M. OCTOBER 7

I don't have to go far to get to a desolate place.

Meanwhile, out of the void, days spring like fungi, like stubby and nailless pale fingers. Idly, I twist their tips. The form stays.

sunrise 292
6:48 A.M. OCTOBER 8

I lifted the sheer, and what I saw was unlike my blurred and shining concept of "sunrise," which persists. I dropped the curtain, startled. *Dawn* is honester, at least.

sunrise 293
6:49 A.M. OCTOBER 9

Pour a bowl of pallor.

Light
piles like
sand, like sentences
to speak later, like stalagmites,
announcing. No translatable content,
only plasma, noun, will, demand/desire, convexity.

sunrise 294
6:50 A.M. OCTOBER 10

Four-note meadowlark, hey! Hey! Four-note
meadowlark, hey!

sunrise 295
6:51 A.M. OCTOBER 11

I can last it. I can outlast it.

sunrise 296
6:51 A.M. OCTOBER 12

Tuck the sheets and blankets under. Crinkling pages, aging, curl at the edges. Ask for the full story, and certain spans of its perimeter fold under or up, curling unwanted details away. Day curls under at its edges.

sunrise 297
6:52 A.M. OCTOBER 13

Out in the hall, I don't look up. I wouldn't
see the ceiling, only high, high blackness and
golden falling flares. Maybe you've seen this
in movies. I must have. My glance catches
the window, and I check the time. The
morning's overcast. The flames sizzle soft at
the tops of the clouds.

sunrise 298
6:53 A.M. OCTOBER 14

I was up most of the night. Sunrise wasn't the event at six,
        six-thirty;
    finishing work was—finishing work and eating the sorry
French toast. Outside the sky was brittle. No effervescing:
        I know it. I'm scavenging.
        Join me?

sunrise 299
6:54 A.M. OCTOBER 15

Rusted, wet.

sunrise 300
6:55 A.M. OCTOBER 16

The two mounds of white sugar were starting to mix.

The man denied his name in order to escape.

No one could assign the children rightly to their places.

sunrise 301
6:56 A.M. OCTOBER 17

o rolling east, o scratched-up plastic, o hazy
pink space between sense and knowing, again
between knowing and saying,

o chill, o walnuts silhouetted,

sunrise 302
6:57 A.M. OCTOBER 18

Message (if there is one, if a delivery's
coming today) exhibits its veracity
(and thereby its teeth) not by battering,
   hammering, storming down the door—rather,
      by stealing in, yea, infiltrating:
                  winds around corners,
                        gains entrance,
                  and we are entranced.

sunrise 303
6:58 A.M. OCTOBER 19

Observed and observer meet within the observer.
Get a good look around,
and they'll meet
within the observed.

sunrise 304
6:59 A.M. OCTOBER 20

Room 304 didn't have any windows.

sunrise 305
6:59 A.M. OCTOBER 21

To speak of fearlessness is to acknowledge
some cause for fear.

Nothing's alabaster here.

Basted and bested, we stare (up and outward), dumb and alert.

You know well what the limits are, where
they are, and where they're secured on dis-
play. Tie yourself tangled in caution tape.

sunrise 306
7:00 A.M. OCTOBER 22

I want to be sharpened. Surely I live among whetstones. They must be disguised. For when I look around, most of what I see threatens either to crush me by blows or to (over years) sand me down and away.

sunrise 307
7:01 A.M. OCTOBER 23

So load me down with epiphanies, unwieldy and hot though they be. Eclipse the far sun with some small projectile. I'm off to draw water. Barefoot and balanced, I'm plenty alert; I'll wend my way around sharp stones and shards of broken glass.

sunrise 308
7:02 A.M. OCTOBER 24

Far back on the mountain, a pack of orange trees catches the light, gold-thrumming as the forsythia. I'm dreaming. Forsythia's long out of bloom.

7:08: still up before the sun, which someone's kicked south. 7:13: a birth—it's wriggling, wrestling its bright, bullish way over the horizon, out over the trees.

Orange leaves line the gutters.

sunrise 309
7:03 A.M. OCTOBER 25

We're tied down with wet thread.

The thunder-full night stole the blaze from the morning.

sunrise 310
7:04 A.M. OCTOBER 26

Out southeast, a battle: a blue knight,
　　with blue shield, sword, and lance, wrestled
　　　　a golden-red animal-angel, large, many-limbed,
　　　　　unpredictable, strong.
They fought above rooftops, between taller towers,
there in a break in the skyline.
　　　　Finally, rain.

sunrise 311
7:05 A.M. OCTOBER 27

These orbiting objects are all roughly
spherical (Their spinning has spun them so,
　　　　　worn down as sea glass.);
　　the orbits are elliptical;
and as for rotation, I understand
　there is some wobbling,
rendering attempts at calculation
　　　　　　imprecise.
So there are no circles here.
We know them by their ordering,
　　　　as we might know
　　　a s i e v e by s i f t e d f l o u r .

sunrise 312
7:06 A.M. OCTOBER 28

oriented: situated

orient: to arrange facing east

(Take a seat.)

sunrise 313
7:07 A.M. OCTOBER 29

My own breath is a lever (tilting, prying), lifting.

The day's got some leverage.

sunrise 314
7:08 A.M. OCTOBER 30

Inertia is orbit and a wide wooden floor. "Sunrise" is high windows, and easing—and easing—

sunrise 315
7:09 A.M. OCTOBER 31

In another story, the sun (They call it "the" sun.) rises every day, not from the horizon but from the center of a flat, flat earth, floating upward like a bubble, pushing through the surface, and by nightfall, disappearing upward from sights, like a balloon. A slow-motion film, played backward, of a drop falling into a wide and cylindrical bucket of water, would show you something of the shape of this daily phenomenon. It is probably not the same ball that tears through the crust of the pancake-flat-earth every day, but everyone speaks as if it is.

Naturally, no one can satisfactorily, airtightly explain how the sun gets from its impossible disappearing height every night back to the fabled under-earth caves.

sunrise 316
7:10 A.M. NOVEMBER 1

A few orange and blue skies, a bluebird of those hues, and now this dress.

I did not ask for these colors to stand as pillars; I did not ask for this to be my frame—but it was so sweet, and so I did ask. And now I am carrying them; now I am balancing them, balancing (high up!) between them. Now this blue is blue-gray, and this orange is gold, and they grip me and spin me; I let them.

sunrise 317
7:11 A.M. NOVEMBER 2

Before we fall silent for lack of songs or lack of answers, before we wake enough to ache—

sunrise 318
7:12 A.M. NOVEMBER 3

Mists like these will tell our secrets—Prisms tell the secrets, explicating light.

sunrise 319
7:13 A.M. NOVEMBER 4

These windows steam easily. I haven't seen frost yet. I might well've missed it. Well. The moon vine hasn't bloomed in some time—not that I blame it. Purple buds swell slow, dark and unwilling, reluctant; that's all.

sunrise 320
7:14 A.M. NOVEMBER 5

About half its leaves are gone now; the vine's winding dry.
But the leaves left are dark emerald and healthy—
or pale green and healthy and new—yes,
November, and they're new!
Not even clinging, but spiraling
up into nothing,
and not even falling.

sunrise 321
7:15 A.M.   NOVEMBER 6

Is quietness key? I will wait for the sunrise
all day.

There: a black towerlike rock, covered in
names scrawled in white.

sunrise 322
6:16 A.M.   NOVEMBER 7

Inside and down,
   there lies a live wire.

Up above ground, boulders
   crumble and rumble and spread.
Clay boulders cover the cracks and spread
   outward, heavy and hefty and damp.

Brush the crumbs away.
   Brush (cleanly, detonate)
       the raging, rambling,
    broke broke broken down debris away,
  and let the buried live taut fiery strand (source)
    rise;
   rise and rule.

sunrise 323
6:17 A.M. NOVEMBER 8

Everyone, down to the caves by the water!

Taking the heat was easier than this—than leaving the oven door open to warm the kitchen, steaming the windows as I pour the coffee.

Now we bury ourselves in the night. Each in his alcove, we duck back and hide, under-cover and under the covers.

Everyone, down to the caves, hollow-yawning for cold blinding-bright water!

sunrise 324
6:18 A.M. NOVEMBER 9

Daylight Saving Time ended Sunday. For months how we've scrimped and saved! All winter now we'll be digging in—whole cold scoops of early light, fat spoonfuls of glisten-ing morning.

The whirling world spins steep, gets away; we reword what we mean in attempts to keep it all on a tight-enough leash.

sunrise 325
6:19 A.M. NOVEMBER 10

Industrial chimneys gleam gold.

sunrise 326
6:20 A.M. NOVEMBER II

First caught sight of the sun in a reflection
off a bar's windows—an altar to the Unknown God.

We are all too nonchalant.

sunrise 327
6:21 A.M. NOVEMBER 12

Out on the window's ledge, the wild vine's
palmate leaves glare, living, lit, translucent.

Morning—all's well.

I have not sighed at beauty in a long, long
time.

sunrise 328
6:22 A.M. NOVEMBER 13

As you fly, you are moving over land that
possesses a varying rotational velocity. You
may pay attention and thus keep in sync
with it, but you may not charge ahead, air-
borne, in a straight line. The world will not
wait for you; it will take no pains to catch
up.

sunrise 329
6:23 A.M. NOVEMBER 14

Awake, and arranging faceted glass bottles on stained wooden shelves.

Awake, and arranging chunks of brick and of light, handfuls of gravel, bloody soon-to-be-scars, burned-out chandeliers.

sunrise 330
6:24 A.M. NOVEMBER 15

First cold fog. So the sun rose in a mug of coffee, and in the yellow, yellow headlights of the cars. It rose in small plugged-in appliances. It rose curtly, kindhearted, recursively.

So pack up and go (winter coat slung across your right shoulder), ford fury, and swallow the capsule of pale parenthetical catch-all.

And have a good day.

sunrise 331
6:25 A.M. NOVEMBER 16

Rain, and waiting.

sunrise 332
6:26 A.M. NOVEMBER 17

Heater off, secrets told. Desire: sold, away
down the cold river.

sunrise 333
6:27 A.M. NOVEMBER 18

Before six, purple, which faded to pale gray-
violet, which faded to pale-violet gray, blank
and cold.

Truncated screeching repeats—fire alarm in
the high-ceilinged hall demanding virgin al-
kaline. I could use a ladder.

The sun's slipped out past the clouds, plans
to spend the day upstairs. I have not been invited, but I would climb up and see.

Some days, with the gnostics, I would climb
up on out of the world if I could.

sunrise 334
6:28 A.M. NOVEMBER 19

A ray needs a departure point and a direction. Specificity loves a nail; I'm partial to
open endings.

Night lies raveled at our feet.

sunrise 335
6:29 A.M. NOVEMBER 20

We create a vaster space when we speak, if we speak well—if we keep soft and silent, speaking only to clarify, only to build: rhinestones, tapestries, twisted iron columns, red bricks.

You say you're cold and hungry. I'll conjure up a feast if we can but agree.

Sunlight slides over the top of the curtain.

sunrise 336
6:30 A.M. NOVEMBER 21

Pare down, pare down, pare down.

sunrise 337
6:31 A.M. NOVEMBER 22

sun-born: stubborn & stampeding rampant rose

sunrise 338
6:32 A.M. NOVEMBER 23

I can show you the sunrise, but all we have here for breakfast are color, authority, cups of cold water.

sunrise 339
6:33 A.M. NOVEMBER 24

As I sat at the table, waiting for coffee, I saw I was hunched over, slouching for warmth. I straightened up, opened my chest, and felt warmer (perhaps at the friction between the insistent up-moving will and the hideaway stay-warm inertia).

The fury of orchid and orange will surrender within the next hour, maybe even half, but not without having its say.

sunrise 340
6:34 A.M. NOVEMBER 25

I can see into the future, as the horizon's atmosphere-molecules refract the image of the rising sun in my direction.

sunrise 341
6:35 A.M. NOVEMBER 26

Some mornings the small lit wick flickers, blinks.

Dawn was all fire and roses. In the sky just above the horizon, I can see farther than land's end, straight horizontal into farther sky. At the horizon the world is tilted so that its secrets escape. At the horizon we've tilted it, angled it squinting, as if we mean to look down into a treacherous tube or into a promising jar.

sunrise 342
6:36 A.M. NOVEMBER 27

The surface is covered in tall clay jars, jars
with squat bellies, long necks. We're each
down inside one. We're each of us waiting.
What we have here are vessels and waiting
and wanting. What we have here are vessels
and wanting and waiting for light. What we
have here are little people and wanting and
waiting for direct light. The span of each life
poses a question, and/unless the span of
each question poses a life.

sunrise 343
6:37 A.M. NOVEMBER 28

The first frost fell sometime back; this was
the first frost fat on the windshield, first icy-
slick frost on the back stairs.

The sun rises over the city and over the ice,
biding or biting the time.

sunrise 344
6:38 A.M. NOVEMBER 29

Controlled communication with the world
yields regimented Beauty, as a Sieve.

sunrise 345
6:39 A.M. NOVEMBER 30

Blue haze, cold mud: occasion for sculpture,
for stuttering naming, for song.

sunrise 346
6:40 A.M. DECEMBER 1

: one

[the city groans.

the brain conjures visions, solutions; the neu-
rons chant spells. well. their efficacy's illu-
sive as elusive's their fruition.

"December!" just remembered—the realization concomitant with an image of a snow-
flake forming, appropriate to, you know,
realization—that inner & cranial crackle: ex-
plode, welcome, adjust]

: "one"

[a precarious and ultimate trust]

sunrise 347
6:40 A.M. DECEMBER 2

another wide pearl (bold, bald, clouded over)
to swallow.

sunrise 348
6:41 A.M.   DECEMBER 3

Before dawn, you can see this is a jagged fortress (Walls and light bulbs make it habitable, identifiable, yet more desolate than hospitable.); you can feel behind you a vast, westerly plain. [When Dawn eases in, watch her: she won't shiver.]

sunrise 349
6:42 A.M.   DECEMBER 4

Look: it's dark, dark and white.

And the candles (standing lit along the hearth & mantel) can't hold candles to the explosion of a day I keep expecting.

sunrise 350
6:43 A.M.   DECEMBER 5

Chimes instruct the morning.

sunrise 351

Suppose I'm a compass; then I'm a compass that needs to be
    wound.
I've come fitted with gears that slow,
          hands that hesitate,
        hung up on the numbers.
I don't show direction any better than I keep the time.
    (Oh, but I keep the time—
some under my tongue, some up in the closet, some locked up
    in boxes, a chip of it set in a ring.)
I come down the stairs, and the sun's done run off,
                done run south.

sunrise 352

Clouds rise in looming and luminous swells.

sunrise 353

The four-note meadowlark has not flown south.

sunrise 354
6:46 A.M.   DECEMBER 9

The apartment is high-ceilinged and cold. The pink fire-hazard blanket is on, set to 6. Orbitally, we're closer to the sun than we were in the summer; hemispherically, we're lifting our noses and chins back and up, posing so, in cautious so-convince-me hesitation (in the cold).

sunrise 355
6:47 A.M.   DECEMBER 10

Wishful bargainers, line up, line up by the window. Dawn's foregone.

Lie back, world: forego finality of dark for that white exploding gold.

sunrise 356
6:48 A.M.   DECEMBER 11

This morning, before dawn or anything happened, the security lights that top every near bar and hotel shone without their typical glaring acerbity—but with, or as if with, serenity. The atmosphere was unusually soft—muted light, and muted darkness, too. Through this I regarded the shabby, stately, misshapen neighborhood edifices with—was it compassion? For edifices?

The air is soft, and the town's in a trance or else has gone spelunking.

sunrise 357
6:49 A.M. DECEMBER 12

When I woke, it was already snowing.

Sometimes I visualize lines or strings connecting me (usually by the brain, every once in a while by the heart) to other things. Stars, people, exits, flowers, cars, outer corners. Tried it with snowflakes.

sunrise 358
6:49 A.M. DECEMBER 13

I knew there would be ice. I'd figured there'd be ice eventually. Weeks ago, the kitchen windows started steaming in the morning, then standing all day wet. The indoor ice warmed me (heart, knower, guts, noggin), so wintry hard and definite, crinkling all the outdoor light.

While the kettle boiled, I sat on the floor, tearing at a tangerine.

sunrise 359
6:50 A.M. DECEMBER 14

We'll hit the solstice in a week.
My hands and brains are so full
        that I'll have to start now,
                        easing
                        one book,
                                mug,
                        pen,
                                scarf,
                        bottle,
                odd bag down to the floor at a time.
        "Cast away, O woman,
                whatever impedes the appearance of light."

sunrise 360
6:51 A.M. DECEMBER 15

If in words there's some viable vantage—here's a list:

tangent, ice, dim,

adjust, scour, astringent,

filter, infiltrate,

scintillate, orbit, revisit,

vision, fiction, accelerate,

start, stance, distance,

hesitate.

sunrise 361
6:51 A.M.   DECEMBER 16

Enough. Enough. Enough. Love what is near.

sunrise 362
6:52 A.M.   DECEMBER 17

Awake for the dawn, purple and vertical.

sunrise 363
6:53 A.M.   DECEMBER 18

Light seeps through the clouds like blood from a fine scrape, brimming.

sunrise 364
6:53 A.M.   DECEMBER 19

I FELL out of bed, which startled me so much I could do nothing but laugh. The living room door opened; the morning was brilliant.

sunrise 365

From dreams of laughter and strange etymologies, I wake to darkness, and again to light. Photons hit the curling iron, there on the windowsill; photons hit the scratched wooden floor.

Sunrises and words are measured in different units, and I don't know the conversion factor. What's the factor of conversion between seeing and saying? Between being and articulating?

I know I am prone to silence.

When forces within or without threaten to silence and suffocate, stand still at the membrane: that undulating, winding line dividing intuition and desire, risk and necessity, danger and weightlessness, silence and song.

Language, too, is a light. Or else language is another atmosphere, through which light or its analog travels, diffuses, spreads.

There's a total lunar eclipse tonight. If the clouds don't clear, I'm gonna miss it. I'll read Annie Dillard's essay instead. And tomorrow's the Winter Solstice: the base.

sunrise 366

Dawn rose purple and slow.

Ate a grapefruit (sweet, bright), ponderous as stone.

When it was time to go, I climbed down the iron stairs clad in hat, gloves, long wool coat, but the morning air was mild. Instead of ice, I found drops of rain on my windshield. Winterly or not, winter's here. We'll spin on down, lower our proud chin; the sun'll get higher.

The solstice night: bloody, dark, ice-hard; and the day: small, unwinterly, soft. Full circle: night encroaches, turns, recedes; day whispers, widens, gains.

Discipline yields illumination yields freedom.

Persistence concedes humility: Words grow blunt, creak, clatter to the scratched and dusty floor, stripped screws. What remains? An inner solitude, a firmness and openness, an inner turning toward the light, a standing alone on a cliff's edge, palms open, gaze fixed faithfully toward beauty, toward infinity—a steadiness in willingness to be unsteadied and steadied again, balanced by a farther, further force, light not of me.

about the author

ALLISON BOYD JUSTUS' poetry has appeared in *Penwood Review, Nibble, Eunoia Review, Madcap Review, Calliope, Quail Bell,* and *Contemporary American Voices*. A 2015-16 Middle Tennessee Writing Project Fellow, Allison teaches language arts and serves as the gifted education facilitator for Eagleville School. You can find her online at allisonboydjustus.com.

author acknowledgments

The author wishes to express grateful acknowledgement to the editors of the following publications, in which versions of these poems have appeared:

Eunoia Review: Sunrises 1-46
Madcap Review: Sunrise 262
Calliope: Sunrises 256, 257, 258, 264, and 271
Contemporary American Voices: Sunrises 135, 137, and 146

The earliest version of this manuscript appeared as a series of daily posts at solsticetosolsticetosolstice.tumblr.com, public from December 21, 2009, to December 21, 2010.

To all the readers and encouragers of the initial project, thank you.

Thanks to the Middle Tennessee writing community for your brilliance, welcome, and support, and to dear friends and mentors who encouraged this work and the spirit therein—in no particular order: Stefanie Wheat-Johnson, Shelly Tilton, Philip Fairbanks, Nicoll Burleson, Jennifer Gerhardt, Ben Jackson, Jennalyn Krulish, Blake Palmer, Bill Brown, Christine Hall, Lisa Mosier, Ciona Rouse, Kory Wells, Dana Malone, Sandy Coomer, Tricia Schwaab, Poetry in the Brew, Writings on the Wall, Poetry in the Boro, and the Middle Tennessee Writers' Group. To Martha and Charles Taylor (Granny and Pa), thank you for the delicious meals, for the "upper room," and for your love. Heartfelt thanks to the good people of J&J's Market & Café, for a place to be. Thanks to my language arts students for relishing connotation, symbolism, and precision, and thanks to the Eagleville community, especially Marcy Pflueger, I. V. Hill, and the Brouwer family, for your encouragement. To Roy Aderin Justus, my dearest, for your unwavering love and support and so much more, thank you.

colophon

What you are holding is the First Edition of this collection.

The title and subtitle fonts are a combination of Porcelain, created by Misprinted Type, and Dominican Small Caps, created by Harold's Fonts. The back cover Alternating Current Press font is set in Portmanteau, created by JLH Fonts. All other type is set in Calisto MT.

Cover artwork and graphics by Leah Angstman and Michael Litos. The Alternating Current Press lightbulb logo was created by Leah Angstman, ©2006, 2017 Alternating Current. Allison Boyd Justus' photo was taken by Anna Haas, ©2017 Red Hare Photography.

All fonts, artwork, graphics, and designs were used with permission. All rights reserved.

notes on the text

Several lines in this book were inspired by, allude to, or are quoted from Emily Dickinson ("657: I dwell in Possibility," "193: I shall know why"), Henry David Thoreau (*Walden*), *The Astronomical Almanac Online*, *The Bible*, Claudius Ptolemy (*Almagest*), Amaryllis Place ("Life Cycle of a Star"), Annie Dillard ("Total Eclipse"), Jean Mermoz (within Antoine de Saint-Exupéry's *Wind, Sand, and Stars*), University of Southern California on Phys.org ("'Sloppier Copier' Surprisingly Efficient"), Julian of Norwich, Maurice Sendak (*Outside Over There*), and C. Alex Young (*The Sun Today*).

other works

FROM ALTERNATING CURRENT PRESS

All of these books (and more) are available at Alternating
Current's website: press.alternatingcurrentarts.com.

alternatingcurrentarts.com

Made in the USA
Middletown, DE
20 January 2019